Rigor in the K–5 Math and Science Classroom

Learn how to incorporate rigorous activities in your math or science classroom and help students reach higher levels of learning. Expert educators and consultants Barbara R. Blackburn and Abbigail Armstrong offer a practical framework for understanding rigor and provide specialized examples for elementary math and science teachers. Topics covered include:

- ♦ Creating a rigorous environment
- ♦ High expectations
- ♦ Support and scaffolding
- ♦ Demonstration of learning
- ♦ Assessing student progress
- ♦ Collaborating with colleagues

The book comes with classroom-ready tools and are offered in the book and as free eResources on our website at www.routledge.com/9780367343194.

Barbara R. Blackburn, a Top 30 Global Guru in Education, has taught early childhood, elementary, middle and high school students, and has served as an educational consultant for three publishing companies. In addition to speaking at international, national and state conferences, she also regularly presents workshops for teachers and administrators in elementary, middle and high schools. She is the author of numerous books, including the bestseller *Rigor Is Not a Four-Letter Word.*

Abbigail Armstrong, co-author of *Rigor in the 6–12 Math and Science Classroom*, is a professor at Winthrop University, teaching undergraduate and graduate courses in the Middle Level Education Program. She supervises middle school student teachers and collaborates with area schools on special projects. She regularly presents on student motivation, rigor and high-impact instructional strategies nationally.

Rigor in the K–5 Math and Science Classroom

A Teacher Toolkit

**Barbara R. Blackburn and
Abbigail Armstrong**

Routledge
Taylor & Francis Group

NEW YORK AND LONDON

First published 2020
by Routledge
52 Vanderbilt Avenue, New York, NY 10017

and by Routledge
2 Park Square, Milton Park, Abingdon, Oxon, OX14 4RN

Routledge is an imprint of the Taylor & Francis Group, an informa business

Library of Congress Cataloging-in-Publication Data
Names: Blackburn, Barbara R., 1961– author. | Armstrong, Abbigail,
    author.
Title: Rigor in the K-5 math and science classroom : a teacher toolkit /
    Barbara R. Blackburn and Abbigail Armstrong.
Description: New York, NY : Routledge, 2020. | Includes bibliographical
    references.
Identifiers: LCCN 2019035232 (print) | LCCN 2019035233 (ebook) |
    ISBN 9780367343170 (hardback) | ISBN 9780367343194 (paperback) |
    ISBN 9780429324994 (ebook)
Subjects: LCSH: Mathematics—Study and teaching (Elementary) |
    Mathematics—Study and teaching (Kindergarten) | Science—Study
    and teaching (Elementary) | Science—Study and teaching
    (Kindergarten) | Motivation in education.
Classification: LCC QA135.5 .B537 2020 (print) | LCC QA135.5 (ebook) |
    DDC 372.35/049—dc23
LC record available at https://lccn.loc.gov/2019035232
LC ebook record available at https://lccn.loc.gov/201903523

ISBN: 978-0-367-34317-0 (hbk)
ISBN: 978-0-367-34319-4 (pbk)
ISBN: 978-0-429-32499-4 (ebk)

Typeset in Palatino
by Apex CoVantage, LLC

Visit the eResources: www.routledge.com/9780367343194

Dedication

We dedicate this book to those who love their content areas and teach with a passion to enhance student learning.

I dedicate this book to my former graduate students at Winthrop University. Each of you had talents and insights, which you used to make a difference with your own students every day. —*Barbara*

I dedicate this book to my husband Jerome for supporting and loving me and always saying, "you can do this!"

I also dedicate this book to the loving memory of my mother Sarah Jefferson who taught me that obstacles are just tools to build strength. —*Abbigail*

Contents

eResources

As you read this book, you'll notice the eResources icon ⬢ next to the following tools. The icon indicates that these tools are available as free downloads on our website, www.routledge.com/9781138302716, so you can easily print and distribute them to your students.

Bonus Resource Not in the Book: Facilitator's Guide for Book Studies

Meet the Authors

Barbara R. Blackburn, named a Top 30 Global Guru in Education, has dedicated her life to raising the level of rigor and motivation for professional educators and students alike. What differentiates Barbara's twenty-one books are her easily executable concrete examples based on decades of experience as a teacher, professor, and consultant. Barbara's dedication to education was inspired in her early years by her parents. Her father's doctorate and lifetime career as a professor taught her the importance of professional training. Her mother's career as a school secretary shaped Barbara's appreciation of the effort all staff play in the education of every student. Barbara has taught early childhood, elementary, middle, and high school students and has served as an educational consultant for three publishing companies. She holds a master's degree in school administration and was certified as a teacher and school principal in North Carolina. She received her PhD in Curriculum and Teaching from the University of North Carolina at Greensboro. In 2006, she received the award for Outstanding Junior Professor at Winthrop University. She left her position at the University of North Carolina at Charlotte to write and speak full time.

In addition to speaking at state, national and international conferences, she also regularly presents workshops for teachers and administrators in elementary, middle and high schools. Her workshops are lively and engaging and filled with practical information. Her most popular seminars include:

- Rigor Is NOT a Four-Letter Word
- Rigorous Schools and Classrooms: Leading the Way
- Rigorous Assessments
- Differentiating Instruction Without Lessening Rigor in Your Classroom
- Motivation + Engagement + Rigor = Student Success
- Rigor for Students With Special Needs
- Motivating Struggling Students

Barbara can be reached through her website: www.barbarablackburn online.com.

Abbigail Armstrong, co-author of *Rigor in the 6–12 Math and Science Classroom*, began her public school teaching career in 1995 as a middle school mathematics teacher. She received her doctorate in Curriculum and Instruction from Gardner-Webb University in 2010. Building on her classroom experiences and specializations in math, content literacy and middle-level education, she became a professor at Winthrop University in 2005. She now teaches undergraduate and graduate courses in the Middle Level Education Program. She supervises middle school student teachers and collaborates with area schools on special projects. Dr. Armstrong has worked on several projects involving assessing rigor in schools and program evaluation. She regularly presents on student motivation, rigor and high-impact instructional strategies nationally. She also has a strong background in working with at-risk students, particularly those from a poverty background. She has worked with Dr. Blackburn for more than ten years and is a skilled presenter who brings a real-life, down-to-earth perspective to her presentations. Participants are most excited about her practical approach and hands-on learning experiences.

Acknowledgments

As always, my husband, Pete, is my rock and foundation. He inspires me, encourages me when I am struggling and is the joy of my life. My family—my stepson Hunter; my parents Bob and Rose; my sisters Becky and Brenda; and my brothers-in-law Quinn, John and Anthony—are always supportive of my work. For all my friends who regularly cheer me on, especially my "coffee group." Finally, I'm especially grateful to Abbigail Armstrong, my co-author, my former student, my colleague and my best friend. We've talked about this for a long time, and our dream finally came true.

—Barbara

Always I thank God for being a consistent presence and the root of all of my support. To my children Asheland and Justin for allowing me to steal time away to write. I especially thank Asheland for sharing her elementary school experiences. I thank my family and friends for continuous encouragement and prayers. Many thanks to you, Barbara, for your writing mentorship and for making me a "butterfly" writer.

—Abbigail

From Barbara and Abbigail

To our colleague and friend Melissa Miles, co-author of *Rigor in the ELA and Social Studies Classroom* books (K–5 and 6–12) for her collaboration and input, which improved our writing.

To Ron Williamson, co-author of *Rigor in Your School: A Toolkit for Leaders*, thank you for your thoughts and materials for Chapter 7.

To Brad Witzel, co-author of *Rigor in the RTI and MTSS Classroom*, for his ideas in Chapter 4 related to students with special needs, thank you for your insights.

To Lauren Davis for exceptional work helping us merge two voices together into a unified narrative.

To Andrea Perdue, Tamikia Samuels, Brenda Blasco, Robin Collins, Kym Zamora and Victoria Hunt for the Social Studies adaptation of "Flesh It Out" in Chapter 4.

To Emma Capel, you came through with a flair for the cover!

To Project Manager Autumn Spalding, thanks for making the production process smooth.

Preface

This book springs from feedback we regularly receive during our workshops. Despite a variety of practical suggestions, teachers always want more . . . particularly in their subject areas.

In Chapter 1, we will discuss the data that supports a need for increased rigor in math and science, the myths related to rigor and the definition for rigor. In Chapter 2, we'll focus on the aspects of your classroom environment that support rigor. Here, you'll find topics such as student motivation, growth mindset and developing student ownership. Chapters 3 and 5 are companions: how to increase expectations and how to demonstrate learning that meets those expectations. You may choose to read those together.

In Chapter 4, we'll emphasize the support and scaffolding needed to aid students so they can be successful with rigorous work. This is a critical aspect of rigor—and one you want to pay particular attention to. Chapter 6 details aspects of both formative and summative assessment, with specific examples and suggestions for strategies. Finally, in Chapter 7, we'll provide recommendations for working together with other teachers to improve learning. If you are participating in a professional learning community (PLC), hopefully you'll find some new ideas to consider. If you are considering beginning a PLC, we provide a good starting point.

Our goal is for you to immediately use what you read in this book. Each chapter is organized into smaller topics. At the end of Chapters 2 through 7, you'll find *Points to Ponder*, which will allow you to reflect on your learning. Finally, you can contact us through Barbara's website, www.barbarablackburnonline.com. We would like to hear from you as you implement the ideas from the book. One of the best parts of writing a book occurs when teachers and students share how they took an idea and made it their own. As you read the chapters, we hope you will find ideas that will enhance your classroom. Enjoy the journey to new learning!

1

Introduction

Rigor has been an area of increasing focus in education. However, when you talk with teachers and leaders, everyone seems to have a different understanding of what rigor means, especially what it looks like in the classroom. In this chapter, we'll look at why rigor is important, the misconceptions related to rigor and a clear definition of rigor.

The Call for Rigor

In 1983, the National Commission on Excellence in Education released its landmark report *A Nation at Risk*. It painted a clear picture: Test scores were declining, lower standards resulted in American schools that were not competitive with schools from other countries and students were leaving high school ill-prepared for the demands of the workforce. *"Our nation is at risk. . . . The educational foundations of our society are presently being eroded by a rising tide of mediocrity that threatens our very future as a nation and a people."* More than 30 years later, similar criticisms are leveled at today's schools.

New Calls for Rigor

Since *A Nation at Risk* was released, the call for more rigor has only increased. *The Condition of College and Career Readiness* (2011), a thorough report from the ACT, has reinforced the lack of preparedness by high school graduates for college and for the workforce. According to the 2018 ACT report, "The percentage of students meeting at least three of the ACT College Readiness Benchmarks in the four core subject areas was 38% for the 2018 US high school graduating class, down from 39% last year but the same as in 2016" (p. 2). In 2010, the Common Core State Standards (www.corestandards.org) were created to increase the level of rigor in schools. Other recently revised state standards similarly reinforced the need. Rigor is at the center of these standards, and much of the push for new standards came from a concern about the lack of rigor in many schools today, as well as the need to prepare students for college and careers.

Despite these efforts, results indicate a further decline in the progress of American students compared to that of other nations. Most recently (2017), the Pew Research Center released information that the academic achievement of students in the United States lags that of students in many other countries. As they point out, "Recently released data from international math and science assessments indicate that U.S. students continue to rank around the middle of the pack, and behind many other advanced industrial nations" (www.pewresearch.org/fact-tank/2017/02/15/u-s-students-internationally-math-science/).

Scores on the Program for International Student Assessment (PISA)		
Subject	*Ranking*	*Score Compared to Highest Score*
Math	38 out of 71	470 compared to 564
Science	24 out of 71	496 compared to 556

Source: www.pewresearch.org/fact-tank/2017/02/15/u-s-students-internationally-math-science/

Based on data from the 2015 Trends in International Mathematics and Science Study (TIMSS), students in the United States have shown improvement in mathematics and science scores from 1995 to 2015. Even though scores have improved overall, fourth grade students scoring advanced or high on TIMSS benchmarks is significantly less than the amount who scored at the low level in both content areas. Students who scored in the advanced and high levels were able to understand and apply knowledge when faced with complex situations and concepts, whereas students scoring low only had basic knowledge. In mathematics, only 14% of students scored advanced and 47% percent scored high versus, 95% of students scored low. The data is similar but slightly improved for science scores with 16% of students scoring advanced, 51% scoring high, but 95% of students scored low. Even with improvements in overall scores, students largely are passing with basic knowledge instead of being challenged.

Percentage of Fourth-Grade Students Meeting TIMSS Mathematics Benchmarks in 2015			
Advanced	*High*	*Intermediate*	*Low*
Students can apply their understanding and knowledge in a variety of relatively complex situations and explain their reasoning.	Students can apply their knowledge and understanding to solve problems.	Students can apply basic mathematical knowledge in straightforward situations.	Students have basic mathematical knowledge.
14%	47%	79%	95%
Percentage of Fourth Grade Students Meeting TIMSS Science International Benchmarks in (2015)			
Advanced	*High*	*Intermediate*	*Low*
Students communicate understanding of complex concepts related to biology, chemistry, physics and Earth science in practical, abstract and experimental contexts.	Students apply and communicate understanding of concepts from biology, chemistry, physics and Earth sciences in everyday and abstract situations.	Students demonstrate and apply their knowledge of biology, chemistry, physics and Earth science in various contexts.	Students show some basic knowledge of biology, chemistry, physics and Earth science.
16%	51%	81%	95%

Source: https://nces.ed.gov/timss/

Key Shifts in NCTM Standards

There are various issues in the mathematics classroom that hinder the progress of students. A lack of rigor is one of the issues. In the most recent *Principles to Actions* document, it was stated that two issues facing mathematics classrooms are that students are learning isolated facts and procedures with no conceptual understanding and lower expectations for students who are considered on a lower academic level. NCTM addressed these deficiencies with recommendations of how to shift from a less rigorous curriculum to one that is challenging for all learners.

Mathematics	
Delving Deeply Into the Key Processes and Ideas Upon Which Mathematical Thinking Relies	
Shift	*Explanation*
Focus: Focusing strongly where the standards focus	Focusing deeply on the major work of each level will allow students to secure the mathematical foundations, conceptual understanding, procedural skill and fluency and ability to apply the math they have learned to solve all kinds of problems—inside and outside the math classroom.
Coherence: Designing learning around coherent progressions level to level	Create coherent progressions in the content within and across levels so that students can build new understanding on previous foundations. That way, instructors can count on students having conceptual understanding of core content.
Rigor: Pursuing conceptual understanding, procedural skill and fluency and application—all with equal intensity	Conceptual understanding of key concepts, procedural skill and fluency and rigorous application of mathematics in real-world contexts.

Next Generation Science Standards

Similarly, there are concerns in science. *The Next Generation Science Standards*, written by forty members from the group of twenty-six lead state partners, are based on the National Research Council's *Framework for K–12 Science Education*. The standards were written in response to four concerns.

Four Concerns
1. Reduction of the United States' competitive economic edge
2. Lagging achievement of U.S. students
3. Essential preparation for all careers in the modern workforce
4. Scientific and technological literacy for an educated society

---

The standards reflect seven shifts from earlier standards. Each of these reflects an increase in rigor.

Shifts to Increase Rigor
1. K–12 science education should reflect the interconnected nature of science as it is practiced and experienced in the real world.
2. The Next Generation Science Standards are student performance expectations—NOT curriculum.
3. The science concepts in the NGSS build coherently from K–12.
4. The NGSS focus on deeper understanding of content as well as application of content.
5. Science and engineering are integrated in the NGSS from K–12.
6. The NGSS are designed to prepare students for college, career and citizenship.
7. The NGSS and Common Core State Standards (English language arts and mathematics) are aligned.

Source: www.nextgenscience.org/sites/default/files/Appendix%20A%20-%204.11.13%20Concep tual%20Shifts%20in%20the%20Next%20Generation%20Science%20Standards.pdf

Myths About Rigor

Now that we have discussed why rigor is important in the math and science classroom, let's look at misconceptions about the concept. There are nine commonly held beliefs about rigor that are not true *no matter the content area.*

Nine Myths About Rigor

Myth 1: Lots of homework is a sign of rigor.

Myth 2: Rigor means doing more.

Myth 3: Rigor is not for struggling students or those with special needs.

Myth 4: When you increase rigor, student motivation decreases.

Myth 5: Providing support means lessening rigor.

Myth 6: Resources equal rigor.

Myth 7: Standards alone take care of rigor.

Myth 8: Rigor means you have to quit doing everything you do now and start over.

Myth 9: Rigor is just one more thing to do.

Myth 1: Lots of Homework Is a Sign of Rigor

For many people, the best indicator of rigor is the amount of homework required of students. Some teachers pride themselves on the amount of homework expected of their students, and there are parents who judge teachers by homework quantity. Realistically, all homework is not equally useful. Some of it is just busywork, assigned by teachers because principals or parents expect it. For some students, doing more homework in terms of quantity leads to burnout. When that occurs, students are less likely to complete homework and may be discouraged about any learning activity.

Myth 2: Rigor Means Doing More

"Doing more" often means doing more low-level activities, frequently repetitions of things already learned. Such narrow and rigid approaches to learning do not define a rigorous classroom. Students learn in many different ways. Just as instruction must vary to meet the individual needs of students, so must homework. Rigorous and challenging learning experiences will vary with the student. Their design will vary, as will their duration. Ultimately, it is the quality of the assignment that makes a difference in terms of rigor.

Myth 3: Rigor Is Not for Struggling Students or Students With Special Needs

Sometimes, we believe our students who are struggling—whether they have special needs, are English learners or are challenged with other issues—simply cannot learn at high levels. At times, they cannot answer even basic questions, so we accept that there is a limit to what they can do. Realistically, all students are capable of rigorous work, as long as they have the right support and scaffolding. For example, Dr. Brad Witzel, a colleague of ours, reminds us:

> Just because a student is labeled learning disabled or at risk, it does not mean he or she is incapable of learning. Students with learning disabilities have average to above-average intelligence. Therefore, ensuring their success in school is a matter of finding the appropriate teaching strategies and motivation tools, all of which we can control as teachers.

Myth 4: When You Increase Rigor, Student Motivation Decreases

Because many students do struggle with challenging work, we assume their motivation will decrease. After all, many students already appear to be unmotivated, so what will happen when the work is harder? The truth is that when we "dumb it down" for students, we lessen motivation. They accurately interpret that easier work means we believe they cannot learn, or they become bored, or both. The result is decreased motivation. On the other hand, when we provide challenging work, reflect our belief in their success with our words and actions and provide specific support to help them succeed, they will be motivated to work at rigorous levels.

Myth 5: Providing Support Means Lessening Rigor

In America, we believe in rugged individualism. We are to pull ourselves up by our bootstraps and do things on our own. Working in teams or accepting help is often seen as a sign of weakness. Supporting students so that they can learn at high levels is central to the definition of rigor. As teachers design lessons moving students toward more challenging work, they must provide differentiated scaffolding to support them as they learn.

Myth 6: Resources Equal Rigor

Recently, I've heard a common refrain. "If we buy this program or text-book or technology then we would be rigorous." The right resources can certainly help increase the rigor in your classroom. However, raising the level of rigor for your students is not dependent on the resources you have. Think about the resources you have now. How can you use them more effectively? Do you use a textbook that includes true-false tests? Often, they are not rigorous because students can guess the answer. However, add one step for more rigor. Ask students to rewrite all false answers into true statements, and it requires students to demonstrate true understanding. It's not the resources; it's how you use them that makes a difference.

Myth 7: Standards Alone Take Care of Rigor

Standards alone, even if they are rigorous, do not guarantee rigor in the classroom. Most state standards and the Common Core State Standards are designed to increase the level of rigor in classrooms across the nation. However, they were not designed to address instruction. In fact, they provide a framework for what is to be taught and what students are expected to know. If implemented without high levels of questioning or applications, the standards themselves are weakened. Your instructional practices, or how you implement standards, are just as critical as the curriculum.

Myth 8: Rigor Means You Have to Quit Doing Everything You Do Now and Start Over

Although there may be times you need to create a rigorous lesson from scratch, in most cases, you can take what you are doing and make adjustments to increase the rigor. For example, if you are teaching math, instead of asking students to always solve problems, provide examples of problems that are already solved and ask them to identify the errors. Or, if you want students to read and summarize scientific information, also ask them to generate research questions based on the information.

Myth 9: Rigor Is Just One More Thing to Do

Rigor is not another thing to add to your plate. Instead, rigor is increasing the level of expectation in all aspects of what you are already doing.

For example, if you are working on differentiating instruction, think about how rigor connects. For your lower tiers, it's important to continue to provide rigorous work, although with more support. Rigor is not separate from other components of your classroom, it is a part of them.

What Is Rigor?

You may have heard some of those myths about rigor. But when we delve into what rigor really means, it is focused on student learning.

"Rigor is creating an environment in which each student is expected to learn at high levels; each student is supported so he or she can learn at high levels; and each student demonstrates learning at high levels."

(Blackburn, 2012)

Notice we are looking at the environment you create. The trifold approach to rigor is not limited to the curriculum that students are expected to learn. It is more than a specific lesson or instructional strategy. It is deeper than what a student says or does in response to a lesson. True rigor is the result of weaving together all elements of schooling to raise students to higher levels of learning. We will look at a brief description of each of the core areas in what follows, but we will explore each area in more depth, providing specific activities and strategies, in upcoming chapters.

Discussion of Areas of Rigor	
Chapter	*Area of Rigor*
2	Environment
3	Expectations
4	Support
5	Demonstration of learning

Expectations

The first component of rigor is creating an environment in which each student is expected to learn at high levels. Having high expectations starts with the recognition that every student possesses the potential to succeed at his or her individual level. This doesn't happen when we make comments like "Girls don't do as well in math."

Almost every teacher or leader I talk with says, "We have high expectations for our students." Sometimes that is evidenced by the behaviors in the school; other times, however, faculty actions don't always match the words. There are concrete ways to implement and assess rigor in classrooms. As you design lessons that incorporate more rigorous opportunities for learning, you will want to consider the questions that are embedded in the instruction. Higher-level questioning is an integral part of a rigorous classroom. Look for open-ended questions, ones that are at higher levels of critical thinking. It is also important to pay attention to how you respond to student questions. When we visit schools, it is not uncommon to see teachers who ask higher-level questions. But for whatever reason, we then see some of the same teachers accept low-level responses from students. In rigorous classrooms, teachers push students to respond at high levels. They ask extending questions. Extending questions are questions that encourage students to explain their reasoning and think through ideas. When a student does not know the immediate answer but has sufficient background information to provide a response to the question, the teacher continues to probe and guide the student's thinking rather than moving on to the next student. Insist on thinking and problem solving.

High expectations are important, but the most rigorous schools assure that each student is supported so he or she can learn at high levels, which is the second part of our definition. It is essential that teachers design lessons that move students to more challenging work while simultaneously providing ongoing scaffolding to support students' learning as they move to those higher levels.

Scaffolding for Support

Providing additional scaffolding throughout lessons is one of the most important ways to support your students. Oftentimes students have the ability or knowledge to accomplish a task but are overwhelmed by the complexity of it, therefore getting lost in the process. This can occur in a variety of ways, but it requires that teachers ask themselves during every step of their lessons, "What extra support might my students need?"

Examples of Scaffolding Strategies

♦ Accessing prior knowledge
♦ Asking guiding questions
♦ Chunking information
♦ Foster a collaborative environment
♦ Writing standards as questions for students to answer
♦ Using visuals aids and graphic organizers such as anchor charts or tables to accompany science lessons

---

In Chapter 4, we'll look at subject-specific scaffolding.

Demonstration of Learning

The third component of a rigorous classroom is providing each student with opportunities to demonstrate learning at high levels. There are two aspects of students' demonstration of learning. First, we need to provide rigorous tasks and assignments for students. What we've learned is that if we want students to show they understand what they learned at a high level, we also need to provide opportunities for students to demonstrate they have truly mastered that learning more than a basic lesson. Many teachers use Bloom's Taxonomy or Webb's Depth of Knowledge (DOK). We prefer Webb's DOK for a more accurate view of the depth and complexity of rigor, and we'll explain that more fully in Chapter 3.

Examples of Guidelines for Rigor for Bloom's Taxonomy and Webb's Depth of Knowledge	
Bloom's Taxonomy	*Webb's DOK Level 3*
Analyzing Evaluating Creating **Please note that although the verbs are important, you must pay attention to what comes after the verb to determine if it is rigorous.	Does the assessment focus on deeper knowledge? Are students proposing and evaluating solutions or recognizing and explaining misconceptions? Do students go beyond the text information while demonstrating they understand the text? Do students support their ideas with evidence? Does the assessment require reasoning, planning, using evidence and a higher level of thinking than the previous two levels (such as a deeper level of inferencing)?

Second, in order for students to demonstrate their learning, they must first be engaged in academic tasks, precisely those in the classroom. In too many classrooms, most of the instruction consists of teacher-centered, large-group instruction, perhaps in an interactive lecture or discussion format. The general practice during these lessons is for the teacher to ask a question and then call on a student to respond. While this provides an opportunity for one student to demonstrate understanding, the remaining students don't do so. Another option would be for the teacher to allow all students to pair-share, respond with heads up head down or hands up hands down, write their answers on small whiteboards and share their responses or respond on handheld computers that tally the responses. Such activities hold each student accountable for demonstrating his or her understanding.

Conclusion

The need to increase rigor in our schools is critical if we want to appropriately prepare our students for life after high school, whether that is a postsecondary college, the military or going directly into the workforce. Rigor, however, is more than simply making things harder for students. It is a weaving together of high expectations, scaffolding and support, and demonstration of learning. If we hold our students to high standards and provide them the right support, they will be successful.

2

Creating a Rigorous Environment

One part of rigor that is often overlooked is the classroom environment. However, the culture of a classroom impacts how students work at rigorous levels, if at all. There are five specific areas we can address to create a rigorous environment.

Five Areas

1. Student motivation
2. Growth mindset
3. Building respect
4. Creating safety and security
5. Developing student ownership

Student Motivation

If you've read *Motivating Struggling Learners: 10 Strategies to Build Student Success*, you know that Barbara believes all students are motivated, just not necessarily by the things we would like. Many of our students are not motivated by a desire to learn; rather, they are motivated by the approval of their friends or the wish to earn some money or something else in their lives. To build a rigorous classroom environment, we need to encourage students' intrinsic motivation so they are not totally dependent on outside rewards.

Students are more motivated when they value what they are doing and when they believe they have a chance for success. Those are the two keys: value and success. Do students see value in your lesson? Do they believe they can be successful?

Value

There are many recommendations relating rigor to relevance. That is the value part of motivation. Students are more motivated to learn when they see value or the relevance of learning. Students have a video stream playing in their heads: WII-FM—*What's In It for Me?* When we are teaching, students are processing information through that filter. What's in this lesson for me? Why do I need to learn this? Will I ever use this again?

Ideally, your students will make their own connections about the relevance of content, and you should provide them opportunities to make those connections independently. But there are also times that you will need to facilitate that understanding. There was a first grade teacher who, at the beginning of the year, asked students what their favorite thing to do was. He was beginning a lesson on insects. He asked Shaun, "Why is it important to learn about bugs?" Shaun said, "I don't know, I hate bugs." The teacher said, "Do you like honey?" Shaun got excited and said, "Yes"! The teacher proceeded with some quick information about the importance of bees and bee pollination. Shaun became more motivated to learn because he connected with the importance of a food he liked being sustained.

Real-Life Connections

♦ Measurement attributes: using height and weight to describe themselves
♦ Whole numbers: discovering missing amounts such as how much more money is needed to buy candy
♦ Interdependent relationships and ecosystems: how plants grows from seeds to edible food
♦ Water distribution in the Earth: how much drinkable water we have available
♦ Weather: how to dress for the current weather

Students can also see value in activities and in their relationship with you. When we can provide a hands-on, interactive learning experience, students are more engaged and motivated. Students also find value in their relationships. For example, if you think about your most motivated students, you likely had a good relationship with them. Conversely, with your least motivated students, there was probably not a positive connection. It takes time to build a good relationship with our students, but it is an important part of our role as a teacher.

Success

Success is the second key to student motivation. Students need to achieve in order to build a sense of confidence, which is the foundation for a willingness to try something else. That in turn begins a cycle that results in higher levels of success, both in academic performance and in college and career readiness. Success leads to success, and the achievements of small goals or tasks are building blocks to larger ones.

In Chapters 3 to 5, we'll look at ways to increase rigor in your classroom. Each recommended strategy is designed to ensure your students' success. However, Chapter 4 will specifically focus on strategies to support their new learning and to scaffold growth to increased levels for every student.

Fixed Mindset Versus Growth Mindset

There is a difference between a fixed mindset and a growth mindset. As Carol Dweck explains, a fixed mindset assumes that our character, intelligence and creative ability are static and cannot be changed. A growth mindset, on the other hand, adopts the perspective that our intelligence, creativity and character can change and grow over time.

These two views have a tremendous impact on teaching and learning. If a teacher believes in a fixed mindset, then he or she is saying there is no potential for growth. If a child is intelligent, he or she will continue to be so. If a student is struggling, it's because he or she just isn't "smart enough." On the other hand, if you believe in a growth mindset, you believe that students may start with a certain amount of ability but that can change over time with effort and persistence.

For students, which of these they believe also matters. Students with a fixed mindset typically avoid challenges, feel threatened by others' successes and give up easily. They want to look smart and believe that working hard at a task means they are not smart.

Students with a growth mindset believe they can learn and become better. They embrace challenge, view effort as a positive part of learning and persist through difficulties. Nigel Holmes provides a clear breakdown of the two mindsets discovered by Dr. Dweck. As you read the table, see if you can identify these traits in your struggling learners.

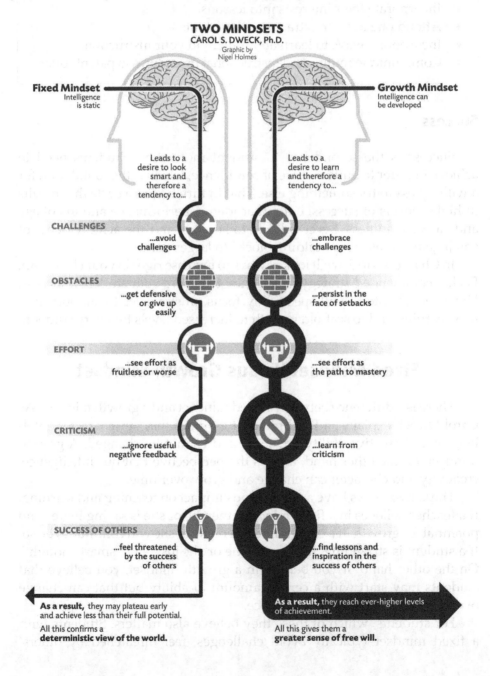

TWO MINDSETS
CAROL S. DWECK, Ph.D.
Graphic by
Nigel Holmes

Fixed Mindset
Intelligence is static

Growth Mindset
Intelligence can be developed

Leads to a desire to look smart and therefore a tendency to...

Leads to a desire to learn and therefore a tendency to...

CHALLENGES
...avoid challenges
...embrace challenges

OBSTACLES
...get defensive or give up easily
...persist in the face of setbacks

EFFORT
...see effort as fruitless or worse
...see effort as the path to mastery

CRITICISM
...ignore useful negative feedback
...learn from criticism

SUCCESS OF OTHERS
...feel threatened by the success of others
...find lessons and inspiration in the success of others

As a result, they may plateau early and achieve less than their full potential.
All this confirms a **deterministic view of the world.**

As a result, they reach ever-higher levels of achievement.
All this gives them a **greater sense of free will.**

Strategies to Develop a Growth Mindset in Your Classroom

A growth mindset is critical to a learning-focused classroom. After all, if you don't believe a student can learn and grow, what difference can you make? During the remainder of the chapter, we'll look at six strategies to develop a growth mindset in your classroom.

Strategies to Develop a Growth Mindset in Your Classroom

- Build a learning-oriented mindset.
- Focus on process as well as product.
- Emphasize mastery and learning.
- Reinforce effort.
- Decrease learned helplessness.
- Provide multiple opportunities for success.

Build a Learning-Oriented Mindset

First, we need to ensure that students have a learning-oriented mindset. Often, they don't. Most of my struggling learners had given up, believing they could never learn. Abbigail shares, "I'll never forget my daughter Asheland stating that mathematics was so hard that she will never be good at it." Asheland, now a middle schooler, has learned that she can be good at mathematics.

Sample Fixed-Mindset Student Statements

- Math is tricky; it's too hard.
- Science is for nerds.
- Math (Science) is only for smart people.
- Only boys are good at mathematics.
- I have never been good at learning mathematics.
- I can get an answer, but I can't give an explanation.
- My hypothesis is always wrong.
- I will never get this.
- Some people are not good at mathematics, and I am one of them.
- My teacher says science is not my strength.

We start the growth by having this mindset ourselves then constantly and consistently reinforcing it with students. We do this by providing the right support for them to learn, encouraging them along the path and celebrating their resilience and success.

Focus on Process as Well as Product

Another thing we can do to help students develop a growth mindset is to encourage them to focus on the *process* of learning, not just on the *product*. Many of my students just wanted to "get finished." They wanted to do their assignments quickly, and whether they were right didn't matter. After all, they weren't that smart anyway, right?

We need to help students slow down and focus on what they are learning and how they are learning. We recommend a three-step questioning process for students, which can be used for self-assessment.

Questions to Focus on the Learning Process

Note: Math example provided; science example in parentheses

Before—What do you think you know about shapes (magnets)?
  —What are you unsure about?
During—What questions do you have about quadrilaterals (how magnets attract)?
  —What sources might help you find more information about this concept/topic?
After—Where did you look for help? Who did you ask for help?
  —What strategies helped you complete your work?
  —How were you successful?

Another time to focus on the process is during classroom discussions. Rather than asking a question, stating whether it is correct and moving on, use a roundabout model. For the first round, simply take all possible responses. For the second round, ask students to partner with another student and discuss the responses from the class. They should agree upon the best possible response. In the third round, discuss the partners' picks for the best answer and agree upon an answer. Finally, reflect on the process, with a focus on what helped students decide on the right answer. This takes a bit of time, so you don't need to do it every time you ask a question; just use it periodically.

Related to the focus on process is the strategy of emphasizing mastery and learning rather than grades. Particularly with older students, there is such a focus on "getting an A" that the joy of learning is lost. Or students are so scared they won't make a good grade, they give up before they start.

Ames and Ames (1990) made an interesting discovery about two secondary school math teachers.

> One teacher graded every homework assignment and counted homework as 30 percent of a student's final grade. The second teacher told students to spend a fixed amount of time on their homework (thirty minutes a night) and to bring questions to class about problems they could not complete. This teacher graded homework as satisfactory or unsatisfactory, gave students the opportunity to redo their assignments, and counted homework as 10 percent of their final grade.
>
> Although homework was a smaller part of the course grade, this second teacher was more successful in motivating students to turn in their homework. In the first class, some students gave up rather than risk low evaluations of their abilities. In the second class, students were not risking their self-worth each time they did their homework but rather were attempting to learn. Mistakes were viewed as acceptable and something to learn from.

As a result, the researchers recommended deemphasizing grading by eliminating systems of credit points. They pointed out there were positive results from assigning ungraded written work. They also suggested teachers stress the personal satisfaction of doing assignments and help students measure their progress.

Reinforce Effort

Encouraging and reinforcing effort are particularly critical for those students who do not understand the importance of their own efforts. In *Classroom Instruction That Works*, Marzano, Pickering, and Pollock (2001) make two important comments regarding students' views about effort.

Research-Based Generalizations About Effort
♦ Not all students realize the importance of believing in effort.
♦ Students can learn to change their beliefs to an emphasis on effort.
(Marzano et al., 2001, p. 50)

This is positive news for teachers. First, we're not imagining it—students don't realize they need to exert effort. And second, we can help them change that belief. Richard Curwin describes seven specific ways to encourage effort.

Seven Ways to Encourage Effort

1. Never fail a student who tries, and never give the highest grades to one who doesn't.
2. Start with the positive.
3. See mistakes as learning opportunities, not failures.
4. Give do overs.
5. Give students the test assessment prompts before you start a unit.
6. Limit your corrections.
7. Do not compare students.

Decrease Learned Helplessness

Learned helplessness is a process of conditioning in which student seek help from others even when they have mastered information. See if this example sounds familiar:

A student is asked to draft a research question in science, but he immediately raises his hand. When the teacher comes over, the student says he needs help, so the teacher reads the prompt to the student and reexplains the elements of a research question. The student still doesn't answer the question. Next, the teacher provides the student with a sentence frame for the question but to no avail. Finally, the teacher gives an example of how he might complete the sentence frame by basically writing the research question for the student.

While this teacher's approach sounds justifiable and maybe even familiar, the teacher is reinforcing the student's learned helplessness. This exchange undermines the student's independent ability to write a research question by himself. Other behaviors that continue a student's learned helplessness include an increased time of completion, lack of academic perseverance, refusal to initiate an attempt and general off-task behavior. Thus, once a student has begun a run of learned helplessness, expect to see the behaviors repeatedly. In the scenario above, the student must learn to attend to the teacher's group instruction and attempt to solve problems.

Instead of running to the rescue of students who can succeed without us or even refusing to help such students, it is important to find ways to teach students to gain independence in their problem solving. In other words, find out why the student is behaving in a certain way, and plan a response that best builds academic success and independence. One way to help is to teach students how to learn and succeed without instantly making excuses and asking for help by following these steps.

Steps to Deal With Learned Helplessness

- ◆ Determine if learned helplessness exists.
- ◆ Explicitly model the preferred academic behavior.
- ◆ Teach the student a strategy for displaying the preferred academic behavior.
- ◆ Provide practice for the strategy.
- ◆ Set a cue to remind the student to initiate the strategy.
- ◆ Allow the student to succeed.
- ◆ Facilitate the student's problem-solving strategy.

Let's use the following scenario to discuss each step. In a fourth grade class during the science block, Raphael is working on a scientific inquiry, and he has been asked to compare the differences between the changes a caterpillar goes through versus a tadpole to become an adult; from this he is to derive a question to investigate. He gets frustrated because he is not sure of the point of the assignment. He opens his computer to begin research but decides his interactive notebook would be the best resource. As he starts to open it, he decides he should ask the teacher what to do. However, Raphael hasn't yet begun the assignment. Instead, he rifles through papers and makes grunting sounds of exasperation. The teacher taps Raphael's desk as she walks by. He rolls his eyes and waves his hand high in a frantic motion like one would make to catch a cab during a rainstorm. The teacher, however, ignores him and continues to work with small groups of students. Intermittently, she encourages students who are putting forth effort toward the difficult reading. Raphael, irritated that he is being ignored, yells out, "You don't care about me!" (Note: What might look like an insensitive teacher to a passerby is actually a part of an organized effort by school personnel to help Raphael overcome learned helplessness. In his IEP [Individualized Education Program], school personnel and Raphael's mother agreed to ignore Raphael's outbursts when he does not exert effort toward completion of a task.)

A few minutes after Raphael's outburst, Raphael opens his book and begins to work. The teacher goes over to Raphael, leans down and praises Raphael for attempting the assignment. She then reminds Raphael that she cannot respond to him when he displays such outbursts, let alone when he does not show effort toward the assignment. The teacher also clarifies with Raphael the expectation during independent practice. The teacher spends the next five minutes with Raphael going over the passage so that he understands the information.

Provide Multiple Opportunities for Success

We believe strongly that students should have the opportunity to redo work they do not complete at a satisfactory level. Too often, struggling learners do what they consider their best work, yet it is unacceptable. At the primary grades, we talk about mastery learning, the concept that students continue to learn and demonstrate learning until we know they understand. Giving students more than one opportunity to "show what they know" is critical to building a growth mindset, as well as feelings of success.

Building Respect

A mentor once told us, "Rules without relationship equals rebellion." This couldn't be more accurate when working with teenagers. If you want your students to invest in your content area and place importance on completing your assignments to the best of their ability, you must first establish a strong rapport with them. The next three sections will focus on building classroom norms to begin this process. Let's start with respect. In order to create a rigorous environment, students must feel that there is a mutual respect between teacher and pupil. Everyone wants to feel as if they are treated fairly and equally. This is no different for your students, whether they are in kindergarten or eleventh grade. In order to establish an atmosphere in which respect reigns, consider asking the students to help you build classroom norms—an agreed-upon set of expectations for conduct in the classroom. Ask students how they want to feel when they are in your room. As they brainstorm a list of words, write them down. Afterward, ask them what they can do to ensure that each classmate experiences these feelings while in the room and write down what you will agree to do as the teacher as well. This is a good starting place for a class contract.

Sample Class Contract		
When in this class, I want to feel . . .	*As a member of our community, I can do the following to make this happen.*	*As a teacher, I will do the following to make this happen.*
◆ safe ◆ valued ◆ engaged ◆ intelligent ◆ productive	◆ encourage my peers ◆ validate others' answers ◆ prepare for class and pay attention ◆ avoid insulting an answer ◆ put forth 100%	◆ not tolerate roasting ◆ welcome your opinions ◆ prepare high-interest, stimulating activities ◆ celebrate your successes ◆ provide clear objectives

This student-centered and student-created set of "rules" is more like an evolving, breathing set of guidelines that gives life to the learning community in your room. Shared values and a shared vision will allow your students to grow together, make mistakes together and celebrate achievements together in a mutually respectful atmosphere where everyone is making the choice to be a part of something greater.

Respect

Rapport is crucial.

Establish an environment of encouragement.

Share the vision.

Provide constructive feedback.

Everyone contributes.

Choice is valued and honored.

Trust is built.

Creating Safety and Security

Maslow's hierarchy of needs teaches us that kids need to feel safe and secure before their mental energy is receptive to academic learning. Not only do our students need to see that we respect them; they also need to know that they can trust us. Creating an atmosphere that is full of grace and patience is part of the growth mindset, but it is also critically necessary in leading students to persevere through rigorous material and activities. As educators, part of our job is to invest in the lives of our students by believing in them and pushing them just beyond their perceived limits. Let's look at three strategies for creating an environment that is safe and secure.

Three Strategies
1. Provide risk-free opportunities to learn.
2. Encourage students to take risks.
3. Teach students to learn from mistakes.

Provide Risk-Free Opportunities

The fear of failure paralyzes some of your students. It prevents them from participating in class, sharing responses during reading time or class discussion, or even beginning to attempt your assignment. For many students, it is suffocating to always be under the scrutiny of the red pen, in an environment in which every mistake will be caught and marked and shown no mercy. Where are the opportunities for students to just take a risk and think outside the box? Do those exist in your classroom? Consider some ways in which you can provide relief for your student and let them explore what works versus what doesn't work without a fear of losing points for trying something new. For example, quick writes in the math or science classroom can offer a way for students to put thoughts on paper without being penalized for mechanics and conventions. It is not always necessary to spell every word correctly or have every comma in place, which stifles the thinking process as well as creativity in many reluctant writers. Free up their mental energy to focus on capturing thoughts by giving them a prompt or question and allowing three to five minutes for them to just write with no grade attached. Primary students can draw and do this. For upper elementary, you may also consider allowing students to provide answers anonymously. You can ask a question at the beginning of class, have students record their response on a sticky note or index card and bring them to you with no name or post them in a designated spot on the board. Students will feel safe in providing their thoughts without fear of being wrong and embarrassed. This can also be accomplished using technology, in which case students enter their responses into an app such as backchannelchat.com, polleverywhere.com or mentimeter.com, and the answers are digitally pushed out to the teacher immediately. We'll provide more information on this in Chapter 6, Assessment.

Encourage Students to Take Risks

When students approach a rigorous task, they are taking a risk. Whenever they answer a question, whether in writing or verbally, their knowledge (or lack of) is made visible to those around them. Most students, including your gifted students, do not typically seek out rigorous tasks. They want to complete minimal work, typically to earn a particular grade. If they attempt more than the minimum, working at a level of rigor, it means they are stepping outside their comfort zone. They may or may not be successful, but it is always a learning experience. The first thing you can do to encourage risk taking is to model it for your students. Tell them when you are trying something for the first time and explain that you are nervous. Describe situations in which you have been uncomfortable and share how you adjusted. In both situations, openly reflect about stumbling blocks you experience, including the lessons you learned.

Second, you can provide other models of people who have taken a risk but have succeeded after overcoming obstacles. You are the perfect example because students think that you are smart and may not know of your struggles; however, you may also choose individuals who are specific to your subject area.

Third, recognize and reward students who are willing to take a chance at something new. This can apply to students who simply exert effort to try a new skill or who are willing to do something new, such as lead a small group or share a problem they have solved with the entire class. You might praise them verbally or use reward certificates.

Sample Certificates

Paws for Progress

_____ showed progress

by_____

_____

Signed_____

Praise for a Peak Experience

_____ excelled at

_____

_____

Signed_____

Lighting Up with Effort

_____ put forth effort

toward_____

_____

Signed_____

Owning and Overcoming Mistakes

No matter what you do or what they do to prepare, students will make mistakes. It's part of the learning process. We've learned this as adults, but it is important to continuously emphasize this with students. We've used huge erasers in our classrooms that say, "For really BIG mistakes." It's laughable, but it gets the point across. Stress to your students that, if everything is easy and they never make a mistake, chances are high that they aren't learning or growing. Much more can be learned about individual strengths and weaknesses through failure. As with encouraging risk taking, emphasize to students that acknowledging that you've made a mistake and reflecting on what you learned is an important part of the growth process.

One specific opportunity you can provide to students is to allow them to revisit their formal assessments. When we grade students' work, penalize them for errors and hand the paper back for it to be filed or thrown away, students typically do not learn from their mistakes. One way to do this is to use a reflective tool after students have taken a test. In the sample that follows, students are provided an opportunity to redo their mistakes, but they are also required to identify what caused the mistake.

Reworking Tests

| Name _____ Date _____ ||||||
| Math Test _____ Teacher _____ ||||||
Question Missed	My Original Answer:	My New Solution (you must show your work including all steps):	The Correct Answer:	Why I Know I Have the Right Answer Now:

Why I Missed the Question on the Original Test (circle all that applies):

♦ I didn't understand the question.

♦ I thought I had it right.

♦ I skipped a step.

♦ I studied this, but I forgot.

♦ I had no clue about this.

♦ I ran out of time or guessed.

♦ I made a careless mistake.

You may decide to create a separate grade in your gradebook for assessment revisions. If you want the original text/project grade to remain, require students to make corrections to the graded assessment and give them a quiz grade to represent their capability to address weaknesses and grow from them. Students need time to revisit mistakes in order to overcome them and prevent them from occurring repetitively. This is the essence of rigorous expectations.

Developing Student Ownership

Student ownership is the level in which your students are invested in their own learning. How does ownership increase rigor? When we shift responsibility for learning to students, students take control of their learning, thereby raising the level of content. Do your students have a personal stake in your classroom? If your teaching were a form of government, would it resemble a monarchy, dictatorship or democracy? In order to raise the level of rigor, you'll want to create a democratic environment. This doesn't mean you don't make decisions; rather, you make decisions that build ownership by students. In terms of physical environment, it is better to rearrange straight rows to configure your desks or tables in a manner that promotes and stimulates collaboration. Since your role in a rigorous classroom includes being a facilitator of learning, it's important to allow students to be face to face to make decisions and learn as a group. Create a physical space that encourages interdependence on one another as a community of learners and safe place in which students feel as if they have opportunities for the three components of student ownership: choice, voice and leadership.

Choice

Students deeply desire having freedom of choice. No matter the content area, you can integrate "pause points" in your plans at which students get to choose how, when or what they learn. The options for choice may revolve around adjusting your expectations, the content, support and scaffolding, your instruction, demonstration of learning or assessment, as long as the learning objective remains intact and each task is equally rigorous. Obviously, students do not need choice all the time, but when used purposefully, they appreciate the opportunity to make decisions on behalf of their own learning. You may give them choices in one or all of the areas described in the following chart.

Choice Options: Math		
Solving Problems: Math		
Support and Scaffolding	*Demonstration of Learning*	*Expectations*
Students may choose to . . . ♦ watch a short video on the concept ♦ ask another student to explain ♦ work alone, with a partner or in a small group ♦ do a center activity to provide content support	Students may choose . . . ♦ which strategy they use to solve the problem ♦ how to present final information using the format of their choice (oral or written response)	Students may choose . . . ♦ the resources for foundational knowledge. ♦ how they will approach the problem ♦ the center they want to visit for enrichment
Choice Options: Science		
Research Project: Science		
Support and Scaffolding	*Demonstration of Learning*	*Expectations*
Students may choose to . . . ♦ watch a short video before reading a text to provide background knowledge ♦ listen to excerpts of a speech delivered by your subject or by someone on the topic ♦ take notes online, on index cards, via voice dictation or using a graphic organizer ♦ use layered meaning for understanding ♦ work alone, with a partner or in a small group	Students may choose to . . . ♦ present final information using the format of their choice (video, technology-based options, role-play or debate, research discussion, etc.)	Students may choose . . . ♦ the research topic within certain parameters ♦ the resources for foundational knowledge ♦ how they will approach the topic ♦ research questions if appropriate

Voice

Students want to feel that their voice matters, that you hear them and that you care what they have to say. This is not something that can be faked, as adolescents are true experts in recognizing a lack of sincerity. Ask their opinion. Seek their feedback. Show them that you'll listen. When giving a quiz in class, you can let the class have a say in the format or the date of the assessment. Creating a shared calendar can assist with this process. After getting their feedback on important due dates for other classes, sports or other extracurricular activities such as drama, you work with your students to make a decision together as to what might be the optimal day for the quiz. This can also be used with homework. For example, you might decide to only give homework three nights a week. If students do not want homework on Thursday nights because most of their other teachers give tests on Fridays, you can probably adjust to that decision. You do not need to do this all the time, but if you provide opportunities for them to participate in decision making, it helps build ownership.

You can also allow students to share their voice by asking students to help you design the learning. An excellent tool for this is an adaptation of the KWL model, the KWHL.

KWHL			
K *What Do I Know*	W *What Do I Want to Learn*	H *How Can We Learn It*	L *What Did I Learn*

Notice the opportunities for ownership. Noting what they want to learn helps, but more importantly, this graphic organizer allows students to identify ways the learning can occur. We met a science teacher who used the process as an introduction to a unit on the effects of plastic on our oceans. The students generated ideas such as inviting an environmentalist and someone from a plastics company to debate the issue, interview a local official from a city/town with an ocean, find a nonprofit group that has researched the issue and study their results and view videos or virtual tours on the issue. Their ideas were creative and helped students become vested in the learning process.

Similarly, in a math classroom, when students are asked about learning strategies for a rigorous topic, they may describe options such as playing a game, using Khan Academy videos, talking with a student who is in a more advanced class or using online software to assist with problem solving.

Leadership

There are a variety of ways you can shift the ownership of learning to the students by allowing them to take the lead. First, you will need to shift your role from director of learning to facilitator. You've likely heard the phrase: "Shift from sage on the stage to guide on the side." That's what this entails. It's a change—and one that requires you to release a bit of control and trust your students. You may think, "My students can't handle it" or "They will get out of control." First, you are still facilitating learning and are very involved in the learning process, just in a different way. Unless students are given opportunities to own their learning, they will never be successful in the process. Here are a few examples of how you can release the onus of learning onto your students.

Leadership Options

Expert Groups: Rather than presenting all of the information on a topic yourself, split it into sub-topics, and assign small groups the task of becoming experts on their assigned strand. They will be the teachers for that part of the lesson.

Learning Roles: In cooperative groups, assign a role to each student. As they engage with the learning material (text, video, online presentation, research, etc.), they will each focus on gleaning information from the perspective of their role and come together at the end to share their learning with one another. This places complete ownership on the students.

Reviews: Allow students to conduct the reviews for assessments. Ask them to generate questions that review the content. You may need to use question stems to help them get started. Then, they can rotate asking the questions to each other in small groups. Finally, they can turn these in for review and possible inclusion in your assessment.

Conclusion

It is important that we address the environmental or cultural aspects of our classrooms so that we provide the best opportunity for students to learn at rigorous levels. Student motivation, growth mindset, a respectful attitude, a feeling of safety and security and a sense of student ownership are the environmental elements that can ensure student success.

Points to Ponder

+ The most important thing learned . . .
+ One strategy I want to implement now . . .
+ One strategy I want to save for later . . .
+ I'd like to learn more about . . .
+ I'd like to share with other teachers . . .

3

Expectations

In a rigorous classroom, our expectations set the stage for the learning experience. If we communicate lowered expectancies, students will be reluctant to attempt to learn at higher levels. In this chapter, we'll look at five aspects of high expectations.

Five Aspects
1. Behaviors that reflect high expectations
2. Ensuring rigor in your instructional expectations
3. Deeper levels of thinking
4. Projects and project- and problem-based learning
5. Genius Hour

Behaviors That Reflect High Expectations

Teachers' beliefs, reflected in actions, demonstrate their expectations for their students. In other words, teachers treat students differently dependent on "expectancy," or what they expect. Although the difference in treatment may not be intentional, students notice it and will meet those expectations—no matter how high or low they are (Williamson, 2012).

How do our behaviors reflect our expectations? For example, teachers tend to probe students more if they have high expectations. This sends a clear message that "I know you know the answer, and if I give you hints, you will formulate a reasonable response." Teachers also demonstrate expectations in the types of assignments or activities implemented in the classroom. Abbigail remembers a time when her gifted students participated in thought-provoking activities such as figuring out the rise of a ramp to meet regulation to be fitted on a building, whereas her "general classes" were given drill-and-practice assignments with very little discussion of solutions and perspectives. As described by Robert Marzano (2010), let's look at typical behaviors related to low and high expectations of students.

Differential Treatment of High- and Low-Expectancy Students		
	Affective Tone	*Academic Content Interactions*
Negative	Less eye contact Smile less Less physical contact More distance from student's seat Engage in less playful or light dialogue Use of comfort talk (That's okay, you can be good at other things) Display angry disposition	Call on less often Provide less wait time Ask less-challenging questions Ask less-specific questions Delve into answers less deeply Reward them for less rigorous responses Provide answers for students Use simpler modes of presentation and evaluation Do not insist that homework be turned in on times Use comments such as, "Wow, I'm surprised you answered correctly." Use less praise.
Positive	More eye contact Smile more More physical contact Less distance from student's seat Engage in more playful or light dialogue Little use of comfort talk (That's okay, you can be good at other things)	Call on more often Provide more wait time Ask more challenging questions Ask more specific questions Delve into answers more deeply Reward them for more rigorous responses Use more complex modes of presentation and evaluation Insist that homework be turned in on time Use more praise

Marzano also provides a four-step process for identifying and addressing these differences in expectations. We've added suggestions for each step, which are helpful as you consider how to ensure overall high expectations for your students.

Marzano's Four-Step Process to Identifying Expectation Behaviors
Step 1: Identify students for whom you have low expectations.
Create a three-column chart and label each column High Expectations, Low Expectations, No Expectations. This may be a difficult task, so think of it in terms of when it comes to completing an assignment, who will turn it in early, who will turn it in on the due date with minutes to spare and who will not even bother.
Step 2: Identify similarities in students.
Consider ways your students are similar. Ask yourself, "Do I have similar expectations because of my students' similarities?" "Are my expectations high or low?" The similarities may be skin color, ethnicity, cultural group, sex or gender. This, too, is not an easy task. Discovering our own biases is challenging, but if you confront why you are treating your students differently, you can begin your journey to equity in expectations.
Step 3: Identify differential treatment of low-expectancy and high-expectancy students (see chart above).
Step 4: Treat low-expectancy and high-expectancy students the same.
Choose three behaviors that you discovered you use with students for whom you have high expectations and practice these behaviors for a few days. It may be that you choose to smile at all students. It may be that if any student gives you an incorrect answer, you will give the student process time or time to ask a friend before moving on. Whatever the behavior, keep a log of the behavior and who received the treatment. Also consider technology and apps that can facilitate the change. For example, Random by ClassDojo, Transum Name Selecting App, and Random Student Selector by LiveSchool allow you to call on random students to ensure that you do not limit your choice of students for responses.

Ensuring Rigor in Your Instructional Expectations

In addition to general behaviors related to rigorous expectations, we need to ensure that our instruction is rigorous. Let's look at two common tools teachers use to determine instructional rigor.

Bloom's Taxonomy

Probably the most popular tool used to determine the level of rigor is Bloom's Taxonomy.

Levels of Bloom's Taxonomy

Remember

Understand

Apply

Analyze

Evaluate

Create

We think Bloom's is a good starting point, but we also find a challenge with this approach. We have come to associate Bloom's levels with specific verbs. However, verbs can be misleading. For example, on the base of taxonomy, create is at the highest level. But is that always true? When conducting walkthroughs in a school, we observed a lesson in which students were creating get-well cards for a sick classmate. Is that rigorous? Of course not. The verb is deceptive.

Let's look at examples in math and science.

Mathematics

Analyze the solution for 15 x 6 by explaining how you determined the answer.

In this assignment, although students are asked to analyze their responses, they are really just explaining how they determined the answer. In other words, students are asked to demonstrate understanding rather than to provide an analysis.

> **Science**
> Using a graphic organizer, create a model of the water cycle.

In this primary example, students are asked to create, which is at the highest level of Bloom's Taxonomy. However, when you examine the full assignment, students are simply remembering basic information and using a visual to demonstrate their knowledge. Students are asked to design a way to present their information that may be considered creative but that doesn't mean the assignment is academically challenging. We believe teachers should provide opportunities for students to demonstrate their creative side—but one that is also rigorous.

Webb's Depth of Knowledge (DOK)

We prefer using Webb's Depth of Knowledge as a benchmark of rigor. Webb's DOK has four levels, focusing on depth and complexity.

> **Webb's Depth of Knowledge**
> Level 1: Recall
> Level 2: Skill/Concept
> Level 3: Strategic Thinking
> Level 4: Extended Thinking

As a side note, there is a very popular circle diagram of DOK on the internet. It is a circle divided into quarters, and each section lists verbs for the level. Simplifying the DOK to verbs takes us back to the same problem as with Bloom's. Verbs can be deceptive.

When writing *Rigor in Your Classroom: A Toolkit for Teachers*, Barbara contacted Dr. Webb's office to ask to reprint the wheel in her book. She received a quick and clear response. Dr. Webb did not create the DOK verb wheel, he does not endorse it, nor does he believe it represents the four dimensions. We understand why. The Depth of Knowledge levels are descriptors of depth and complexity that go far beyond simplistic verbs. Instead, let's look at a detailed description of the DOK levels for math and science.

WebbAlign

SUMMARY DEFINITIONS OF DEPTH OF KNOWLEDGE (DOK)

SUBJECT	LEVEL 1	LEVEL 2	LEVEL 3	LEVEL 4
Mathematics	Requires students to recall or **observe facts, definitions,** and terms. Includes simple one-step procedures. Includes computing simple algorithms (e.g., sum, quotient). ***Examples:*** • Recall or recognize a fact, term, or property. • Represent in words, pictures, or symbols a math object or relationship • Perform a routine procedure, such as measuring • At higher grades, solve a quadratic equation or a system of two linear equations with two unknowns	Requires students to make decisions on how to approach a problem. Requires students to compare, classify, organize, estimate, or order data. Often involves procedures with two or more steps. ***Examples:*** • Specify and explain relationships between facts, terms, properties, or operations • Select procedure according to criteria and perform it • Use concepts to solve routine multiple-step problems.	Requires reasoning, planning, or use of evidence to solve a problem or algorithm. May involve an activity with more than one possible answer. Requires conjecture or restructuring of problems. Involves drawing conclusions from observations, citing evidence and developing logical arguments for concepts. Uses concepts to solve non-routine problems. ***Examples:*** • Formulate original problem, given situation • Formulate mathematical model for complex situation • Produce a sound and valid mathematical argument • Devise an original proof • Critique a mathematical argument	Requires complexity at least at the level of DOK 3 but also an extended time to complete the task. A project that requires extended time but repetitive or lower-DOK tasks is not at Level 4. Requires complex reasoning, planning, developing, and thinking. May require students to make several connections and apply one approach among many to solve the problem. May involve complex restructuring of data, establishing and evaluating criteria to solve problems. ***Examples:*** • Apply a mathematical model to illuminate a problem, situation • Conduct a project that specifies a problem, identifies solution paths, solves the problem, and reports results • Design a mathematical model to inform and solve a practical or abstract situation

Revised 2014

WebbAlign

WISCONSIN CENTER for
EDUCATION PRODUCTS & SERVICES

SUBJECT	SUMMARY DEFINITIONS OF DEPTH OF KNOWLEDGE (DOK)			
	LEVEL 1	**LEVEL 2**	**LEVEL 3**	**LEVEL 4**
 **Science**	Requires students to recall **facts, definitions, or simple procedures or processes.** Involves rote responses, use of well-known formulae, or following a set of clearly **defined procedures.** *Examples:* • Recall or recognize a fact, term, structure, or property • Represent in words or diagrams a **scientific concept or relationship** • Provide or recognize a **standard scientific** representation or simple phenomenon • Perform a grade level-appropriate routine procedure, such as measuring length or completing a basic Punnett square	Requires students to make some decisions as to how to approach the question or problem. Involves comparing, classifying, organizing, estimating, ordering, or displaying data (e.g., tables, graphs, charts). Typically involves multiple-step procedures. *Examples:* • Specify and explain the relationship between facts, terms, properties, or variables • Describe and explain examples and non-examples of science concepts • Select a procedure according **to specified criteria and** perform it • Organize, represent, and interpret data. • Interpret or explain phenomena in terms of science concepts. • Make basic predictions for **cause-and-effect relationships**	Requires students to solve problems with more than one possible answer and justify responses. Involves aspects of authentic experimental design processes. Requires drawing conclusions from observations, citing evidence, and developing logical arguments for concepts. Involves using concepts to solve non-routine problems. *Examples:* • Identify research questions and design investigations for a **scientific problem** • Develop a **scientific model for a** complex situation • Draw robust conclusions from observations and experimental data • Cite evidence and develop a logical argument	Requires complexity at least at the level of DOK 3 but also an extended time to complete the task. A project that requires extended time but repetitive or lower-DOK tasks is not at Level 4. Requires students to apply one approach among many to solve problems. Involves developing generalizations from obtained results and formulating strategies to solve new problems in a variety of situations. *Examples:* • Conduct an investigation, from specifying a problem to designing and carrying out an experiment, to analyzing its data and formulating conclusions • Analyze the results of multiple studies on a particular science topic to form an original conclusion about the subject. • Evaluate strengths and weaknesses of an experimental design and develop a revised experimental design.

Revised 2014

Do you see the deeper structure? It's more comprehensive, which provides a strong gauge of the rigor of an assignment. Notice that although Levels 1 and 2 are important, Levels 3 and 4 are considered rigorous.

Throughout the book, we'll provide specific technology resources as appropriate. This list is a sampling of general technology resources that may be used to support rigorous work. However, as with all technology, how you use it matters, as most of these can also be used for low-level tasks.

Technology and Digital Resources for Possible Use to Support Webb's DOK

- Document camera to explain work to other students, justify conclusions, answer research questions and provide evidence
- Interactive whiteboard for demonstrating problem-solving strategies
- Simulation problems
- Virtual field trips
- Virtual manipulatives
- Wiki pages for collaborative work
- Webquests

Moving to Deeper Levels of Thinking

Let's take a look at examples of tasks and assignments that promote deeper levels of thinking—a critical aspect of rigor. Although we will use Webb's Depth of Knowledge (Level 3) as our base, we will also incorporate facets of rigor from other models, such as the Cognitive Rigor Matrix. First, we'll turn our attention to math then science.

Mathematics Examples

Example One: Volume

You must figure out how much cereal will fit into a cereal box without measuring the box. Three responses have been provided, and you must decide which makes more sense. Illustrate or write how you figured out which response made more sense. Justify or support your reasoning as to why the others did not make sense.

There are several characteristics of a rigorous assignment reflected above. First, students are required to recognize and explain misconceptions, which is an aspect of reasoning as they consider the appropriateness of the solutions to the problems. Next, they must verify the reasonableness of their answers and provide a sound argument in support of their response that elaborates on the real-life situations.

Example Two: Mathematical Proofs

Examining reason by writing mathematical proofs is another way to increase the level of rigor in mathematics. As students provide logical arguments for mathematical solutions and examine their own answers for reasonable answers, they exercise their critical-thinking skills. Proofs are usually synonymous with middle and secondary mathematics, but students in upper elementary grades are able to write basic proofs and examine their own reasoning in a way that is similar to the formal proof writing process for older students. You can find ways to demonstrate learning with reasoning in Chapter 5.

Importance of Examining Reason With Proofs

- ♦ Recognize reasoning and proof as fundamental aspects of mathematics
- ♦ Make and investigate mathematical conjectures
- ♦ Develop and evaluate mathematical arguments and proofs
- ♦ Select and use various types of reasoning and methods of proof

---

Source: From www.learner.org/courses/teachingmath/grades3_5/session_04/index.html

If you want to set up a template for students to use as they move through the proof process, one of the simplest ways for students to practice writing original proofs is to use a two-column proof. The left-hand column includes statements used to prove the information, and the right-hand side is the reason or justification for the statement. However, a good starting point for students new to proof writing is for students to respond to prompts or explain their reasoning by submitting an explanation in sentence or paragraph form.

For students who are just beginning to work with proofs, you can prompt them to help them examine their reasoning. For example, let's look at the associative property of addition.

How do you know the associative property $(a + b) + c = a + (b + c)$ works for addition? How do you know it will work for all real numbers? What illustrations or examples did you use to prove that the property works for all addition problems? Explain how this property may work for another operation. Does your answer make sense? How do you know?

Below, you will see an example of traditional proof form of the associative property as written by an elementary student. This method is best used with students who have mastered reasoning and need enrichment.

Statement	Reason (in the beginning, these are prompted by the teacher)
1. $(a + b) + c = a + (b + c)$	1. Given from my textbook.
2. $(5+6) + 3 = 5 + (6+3)$	2. Parentheses have to be added first because of order of operations, $11 + 3 = 14$ and $5+9 = 14$.
3. $5 + (6+3) = (5+6) + 3$	3. I flipped the problem and still got 14 on both sides.
4. $(a + b) + c = a + (b + c)$	4. No matter how I add the numbers, the sum is the same; this is the associative property.

Next, you can ask students to critique proofs, or mathematical arguments. They can critique proofs from other students or samples you provide. For example, you may provide examples of three proofs (reasoning) for a problem and ask students to critique the proofs using a three-statement method. First, you would show students an example of a problem and work through several ways to solve it. Then, guide them through the process of choosing the best option for the solution. Finally, discuss why the other ways of solving the problem were not as strong. Over time, they will be able to use the three-statement method independently.

Three-Statement Method
1. The best answer is attempt number . . .
2. This is because . . .
3. The reason(s) the other attempts is/are not as strong . . .

Additionally, they should regularly assess their own solutions, determining the reasonableness of the proof.

Self-Checking Questions for Proofs

- ◆ Does the proof demonstrate the statement is always true?
- ◆ Does the specification process provide a contradictory model?
- ◆ Is the proof clear and understandable?
- ◆ Does the proof correctly specify each step of the process?
- ◆ Is there appropriate justification for each proof statement?
- ◆ Remember, sometimes you can prove that something is **not true**.

Science Examples

Example 1-Upper Elementary

Using their knowledge of past catastrophic events that have affected the Earth and life on Earth such as earthquakes, volcanic eruptions, weather devastations and asteroid contact, students must predict the next catastrophic event that is likely to occur. They must base their prediction on research from a minimum of three sources other than the classroom text. Additionally, they must justify their prediction using their research and real-life examples and provide information as to how, if at all, people could prevent or lessen the effects of the catastrophe.

In this example, based on the range of events that happen across the world, students must make and justify a conjecture using a logical argument. Because they must research and synthesize information about past events, they are also attempting to generalize a pattern.

In the primary example below, "Planting Seeds," students are provided the opportunity to make a simple hypothesis, make observations and collect data. In addition to comparing and contrasting, students hypothesize how to improve a plant's growth, as well as making connections beyond the lesson to real life.

Planting Seeds

As a group, discuss seeds. Ask students to predict what would happen if they plant a seed. Then, ask each student to plant a seed in the dirt in his or her cup. Place the cups around the room, using different variables such as sunlight and indoor lighting. Ask students to draw a picture in their science journals of what they think will happen. Each day, observe the seeds and draw their current observations in science journals. Discuss as a group what is happening and why. After seeds have sprouted, ask students to compare their plants. Why are they different or the same? Draw this in the journals. Discuss as a class, with answers such as, "mine grew more because it was in the sun." At the end, have each student explain (justify) why his or her plant grew the way it did and why (variables) with a partner and ask the partner to decide if that is correct. Working together, have small groups of students choose someone's plant that did not grow as much as others. Ask them how they would solve that problem. In the whole group, ask students to explain how the variables (such as the sun) would make a difference with something else related to plants (like a garden). Finally, ask students how these variables might matter to something other than plants. You'll need to use specific guiding questions.

STEM Example
Dirty Water Project

Students follow the engineering design process to design and build an original usable device to clean dirty water. Students must justify why their design is more effective than other ones.

Skills incorporated: collaboration; discourse; engineering design process: (1) ask, (2) imagine, (3) plan, (4) create and (5) improve

Content incorporated: water pollution, water filtration, conservation efforts, fractions, multiplication, division, measurement

Source: Full Lesson Plan and Additional Resources: http://teachers.egfi-k12.org/dirty-water-project/

Projects, Project-Based Learning and Problem-Based Learning

Do you remember doing projects when you were a student? We do. Our teachers typically assigned everyone a standard project; we completed them, turned them in and then received a grade. It wasn't very rigorous. Today, teachers use standard projects, project-based learning and problem-based learning. Let's look at how they compare.

Comparison of Types		
Projects	*Project-Based Learning*	*Problem-Based Learning*
Finished product is the focus. Teacher works mainly after the project is complete. Based on directions and are done "like last year."	Student involvement is the focus. Teacher works mainly before the project starts, although some support is provided to students who need it.	Student inquiry is the focus and is based on driving questions developed by students.
Are oftentimes done at home (hopefully independently by the student). Are closed; every project has the same goal (such as create a diorama of a biome).	Are relevant to students' lives or future lives. Are based on driving questions developed by the teacher that encompass the learning and establish the need to know. Are open-ended projects; students make choices that determine the outcome and path of the research (such as design a fortification that would take your community through a bio-attack).	Are open-ended projects; students make choices that determine the outcome and path of the research. Project is student directed, with the teacher providing support as needed (but typically in a guidance role).

Source: Adapted from a blog entry by Terry Heick at teachthought.com

Project-based and problem-based learning are more rigorous than a standard project, in part because more responsibility and ownership is shifted to students. Additionally, project- and problem-based learning usually require a more advanced level of thinking.

Let's look at additional samples of project- and problem-based learning activities for each grade range and subject area.

Math		
Project	*Project-Based Learning*	*Problem-Based Learning*
Kid's World Extreme- Students use area and perimeter to design a theme park in which each step is outlined and all student projects will result in the same product. For example, the theme park is to include six rides, two restaurants, twelve bathrooms and two entrances and exits (all with dimensions decided)	Students use the same skills to design a theme park, but they decide which items will be in the theme park along with dimensions. Students must explain why they chose those particular items.	Students choose an issue with theme parks that may need to be addressed. This may include having a friend in a wheelchair, ensuring safety for younger children, creating a special space for grandparents or accommodating service animals. Keep in mind that if these changes are already in place, students should evaluate their effectiveness and suggest any changes.
Science		
Project	*Project-Based Learning*	*Problem-Based Learning*
To explore the effect the sun's temperature has on the Earth, students complete a greenhouse effect project in which they build a greenhouse from a set of directions and answer prescribe questions such as: What happens to the temperature of the thermometer? Why do you think the air temperature changes?	Create a presentation (format of choice) to explain a climate-related issue such as icebergs and the rate at which they are melting.	Choose a specific issue relating to changes in the Earth's environment such as the greenhouse effect or sun's effect on Earth. Create a question related to the issue and then create and complete an activity or experiment to answer your questions.

> **STEM Project-Based Learning Example: Coding a Lego Maze**
>
> Students in collaborative groups use coding to build directions for how to get out of a Lego maze. The activity is appropriate for all elementary students, even kindergarten students. They may not be able to use computer language to develop code, but they are able to count and use directional words like left, right, up and down to map out how someone is to escape the maze.
>
> Skills incorporated: collaboration, discourse, critical thinking
>
> Math and science content incorporated: numbers, patterns

Source: https://researchparent.com/coding-a-lego-maze/

Notice that in the problem-based learning examples, students drive the topic. Although general guidelines are provided, such as developing a PR plan, students determine what and how they present that information. In what follows, we've provided additional resources for your content areas. Remember, check the information to be sure it moves beyond simple projects.

> ### Resources for Mathematics
>
> **Problem-Based Learning Search Engine**
> https://robertkaplinsky.com/prbl-search-engine/
> Search engine for math problem-based learning
>
> **Learn With Two Rivers**
> www.learnwithtworivers.org/problem-based-tasks-in-math.html
> Videos on problem-based tasks and sample lesson plans (K–8)
>
> **My PBL Works Buck Institute for Education**
> https://my.pblworks.org/projects?f%5B0%5D=grade_level%
>   3A579&f%5B1%5D=subject_projects%3A77
> Standards-aligned project ideas for grades K–12 for all mathematics, science and other content areas
>
> **K–12 Math Projects: About Project-Based Learning**
> www.ct4me.net/math_projects.htm
> Resources for project-based learning with technology integration
>
> *Problem-Based Learning: An Inquiry Approach* (John Barell, Corwin, 2006)
> A book that takes an integrated approach to problem-based learning. This is beneficial for all content areas.

Resources for Science

Interactive Simulations
http://phet.colorado.edu/en/for-teachers/browse-activities
Interactive simulations of physical phenomena with inquiry-based
activities, searchable by grade level and topic of various topics

The Global Water Sampling Project
www.k12science.org/curriculum/waterproj/
Read about the project and learn how to simulate it with your students or in your community. Designed for grades 6–12, but upper elementary students may be able to complete parts of the project.

United States Environment Protection Agency
https://www3.epa.gov/safewater/kids/index.html
Lessons, games and activities involving pollution for grade levels K–12

Problem-based learning: An inquiry approach (John Barell, Corwin, 2006)
A book that takes an integrated approach. This is beneficial for all content areas.

Source: Compiled using Intel Teach Elements: Inquiry in the Science Classroom, Intel Corporation (2012), and other sources

Genius Hour

Genius Hour is an excellent way to enhance problem-based learning. Genius Hour is inspired by Google's efforts with their employees, where 20% of employees' time is motivated by passion and curiosity. They found that their employees were happier, more creative and more productive. Educators have adapted this for use in a classroom, shifting to the concept of providing students one hour to work on their passions. When we apply this with students and allow them freedom to design their own learning and explore their own interests, it increases an intrinsic sense of purpose. Many schools are now implementing Genius Hour, which occurs for a minimum of one hour per week. Key principles of genius hours are that students take charge of their own learning, including the design of the task, use of inquiry to navigate learning and the creation of a finished product to demonstrate a deep understanding of their topics.

However, some common mistakes can derail a successful genius hour experience for your students.

Common Mistakes

- ◆ Allowing total choice without providing guidance and support (some structure is needed, particularly as they work on their projects)
- ◆ Assuming you aren't teaching during Genius Hour (you are teaching in a different way, as a facilitator of learning)
- ◆ Forgetting to leave time for processing and reflection (critical to success, this also includes feedback from others and you)
- ◆ Not providing the opportunity to practice the final presentation

---

Genius Hour Based on Students' Interests

Inherent in the philosophy of a Genius Hour is the notion that students' topics are driven by things they value. Although you want to give students the widest latitude possible to choose their topics, you may need to provide some guidance, especially for students who are less ready for independent work. Ideally, your students will develop their own ideas, but you may want to give them some topics to use as a starting point.

"Getting Started" Ideas	
Math Ideas	*Science Ideas*
◆ How to start a business with a fixed dollar amount (lemonade stand with a plan) ◆ Creating a plan to help a family serve a nutritious, budget-friendly meal for a week ◆ Building a plant box to accommodate enough veggies to feed a family of four for one week ◆ Convincing other students that math is useful in real life	◆ What unrenewable resources are you most interested in saving on this planet? ◆ Saving water in a drought ◆ New idea for a robot to help make life better for people ◆ New technology that will solve a problem ◆ How to use recyclable items to make something useful to save the environment

You will likely need to provide structure and support for Genius Hour. The amount and type of scaffolding will depend on the readiness levels of your students. Once students have chosen a topic, they give an "elevator pitch," which is a three-minute talk proposing the idea. They can present this to other students or to you. They can use feedback from the teacher and students to adjust their proposal. Some students will be able to complete this with no additional guidelines. Others may need a graphic organizer to help them plan; for others, you may need to provide small-group coaching.

Guiding Questions for Genius Hour Feedback

♦ What is the overall question you are answering?
♦ What have you done/where are you in the process?
♦ What has changed since you started/since we last talked?
♦ What help do you need from me?
♦ Is there anything else I should know?

The process of investigation is similar, with some students navigating their own learning and others needing some level of guidance and support from you, whether in the form of recommended resources, structured study guides or small-group instruction.

For the final product, all students need the opportunity to practice their presentations. The presentation of the end product also requires varying levels of support based on students' readiness. Interestingly, you may have students who are quite advanced in designing and investigating a topic but who struggle with the final product. Remember that students' readiness or skill levels can change at different stages. That's why formative assessment, which we will address in Chapter 6, is critical.

Technology can provide support for you and your students for projects, project-based and problem-based learning and Genius Hour. Although there are many options, let's look at a list of resources to get you started.

Suggested Technology Resources

Kiddle (www.kiddle.co) is a Google search engine developed especially for kids. With visual thumbnails and large Arial font, all search results must meet family-friendly requirements that have been handpicked by Kiddle editors.

Novare PBL Platform is a project management tool that uses narratives, portfolios and learning goals to structure project-based learning.

Prezi incorporates video, audio and other interactive research components for a presentation that keeps everyone's attention.

Project Foundry Project Foundry is a popular learning tool that enables students to plan their own learning and track their progress. It also makes organizing student projects much easier for students and teachers. Schools also love that Project Foundry gives students the chance to build digital portfolios—a necessary skill in today's evolving technological culture.

Scribble Press allows students options to share the work that they've done with others while reflecting on the experience as a whole. Scribble Press allows students to write and illustrate their own books, as well as retelling the story of their challenge-based experience, include final project results and reflect on moments of personal growth.

Wonderopolis (wonderopolis.org) posts wonder questions daily, with researched answers students can listen to with the included audio feature. Some wonder answers are accompanied with video as well; both features are ideal for emergent readers. Students can also ask their own wonders.

Wizard School is an app for iPads or Androids that inspires creativity in very young learners. Formerly known as Wonderbox, the content, developed by educators, contains over 3,000 videos, maps and other content to help students investigate topics of interest.

Conclusion

We often think that high expectations start with our standards. But our behavior toward students is really the starting point. Then, we need to look at criteria for rigorous expectations and samples of tasks and assignments that meet the criteria and provide opportunities for students to respond to high expectations through activities such as projects, project-based learning, problem-based learning and Genius Hour.

Points to Ponder

- The most important thing learned . . .
- One strategy I want to implement now . . .
- One strategy I want to save for later . . .
- I'd like to learn more about . . .
- I'd like to share with other teachers . . .

4

Support and Scaffolding

Many teachers think that the rigor has been "watered down" if we need to support a student in a complex activity. When we ask students to work at rigorous levels, it's critical to provide scaffolding that is intentional and purposeful. Let's face it: Many students are not willing or ready to think critically and deeply unless prompted to do so. Even then, they may not know how to take surface-level thoughts and make them more abstract, creative or complex. When some students perceive that a task is overwhelming or difficult, they shut down before beginning. This is where we help them utilize tools and strategies that will guide them through a mentally challenging academic task. Supporting students and teaching them to approach complex thinking with more confidence and grit will allow all students to access rigorous curriculum. Though the term has evolved over the past few decades, the essence of the word remains the same: Teachers provide temporary learning tools or employ purposeful strategies in progressive stages of student learning, with a gradual release of independence.

How Do I Provide Scaffolding for My Students?

The outdated practice of assigning and assessing work with little to no instruction in between is ineffective. It is also not effective to repeat the same teaching practice over and over again with little to no change in the previous method and expect a different result from students. If you meet students where they are and expect them to achieve at that level and higher, they will succeed but with support in the form of scaffolding. Among elementary students in grades 6 through 12, students will be in different stages of learning, whether that is concrete or abstract, novice or expert. Because of these differences, it can sometimes be difficult to plan for a class of students. Strategies presented in this chapter will help you support your students in a manageable way. Though there are numerous methods for scaffolding, we're going to focus on five key areas. The strategies provided in these areas will engage your students and challenge them while you provide appropriate support. It is important to remember that all students are different and require varying levels of support.

Five Strategies

1. Teaching through modeling
2. Visual tools
3. Deepening understanding
4. Creating a toolbox of strategies
5. Working with special populations

Teaching Through Modeling

One way to teach through modeling is to use explicit modeling. It is important to know that the terms "explicit teaching" and "explicit modeling" are sometimes used interchangeably, but in this chapter we will use the term "explicit modeling." There are also times teachers use "direct instruction," but that is a bit different. Explicit modeling is when you provide a very clear demonstration of the learning process.

Explicit Teacher Modeling

When using the term "explicit modeling," you may think of the phrase, "I do, we do, you do," but there are important tasks during that process that should be considered. Explicit modeling can be summed up in eight essential characteristics or principles.

Eight Essential Components of Explicit Modeling

1. Concept/skill or problem-solving strategy is broken down into its critical features/elements
2. Teacher clearly describes concept/skill or problem-solving strategy
3. Teacher clearly models concept/skill or problem-solving strategy
4. Multisensory instruction (visual, auditory, tactile, kinesthetic)
5. Teacher thinks aloud as she/he models
6. Teacher models examples and nonexamples
7. Cueing
8. High levels of teacher-student interaction

Source: The University of Kansas www.specialconnections.ku.edu/?q=instruction/mathematics/teacher_tools/ explicitly_model_mathematics_concepts_skills_and_problem_solving_strategies

As you review those steps, you may think it is very directive, but explicit modeling is effective for six reasons.

Benefits of Explicit Modeling

1. Teacher as model makes the concept/skill clear and learnable.
2. High level of teacher support and direction enables student to make meaningful cognitive connections.
3. Provides students who have attention problems, processing problems, memory retrieval problems and metacognitive difficulties an accessible "learning map."
4. Links between subskills are directly made, making confusion and misunderstanding less likely.
5. Multisensory cueing provides students multiple modes to process and thereby learn information.
6. Teaching students effective problem-solving strategies provides them a means for solving problems independently and assists them to develop their metacognitive awareness.

Source: The University of Kansas www.specialconnections.ku.edu/?q=instruction/mathematics/teacher_ tools/explicitly_model_mathematics_concepts_skills_and_problem_solving_strategies

Explicit modeling is particularly helpful in math and science classes due to the technical nature of each subject. Modeling may occur in the whole group, with small groups or with individuals. It is particularly effective with step-by-step-oriented tasks such as mathematical tasks that require a series of steps to complete or guiding students through the investigative process. For example, students who are in upper elementary have to perform operations in mathematics that include more than one type of operation and with grouping symbols like parentheses and other types of grouping symbols. The order in which to solve these types of problems can be very confusing and can hinder the problem-solving process. With explicit modeling, the teacher may first introduce each level of operations, demonstrate several examples and then provide examples for students to practice with a partner or individually during a guided practice time. Finally, students are allowed to practice alone with limited guidance in order for the teacher to assess them formatively. Although explicit modeling is considered direct teaching, it is still intended to engage the students and support their success.

As you plan to use explicit modeling in your classroom, keep several steps in mind.

Explicit Modeling Steps

- Make sure students have the appropriate background knowledge and prerequisite skills to perform the task.
- Break down the skill into small learnable segments.
- Make sure the context of the skill is grade appropriate.
- Provide visual, auditory, kinesthetic and tactile ways to illustrate important pieces of the concept/skill.
- Think aloud as you show each step.
- Make the important connections between steps.
- Check for student understanding along the way and remodel the steps that might be causing confusion.
- Make sure the timing is at a pace at which students can follow along but not become bored and lose focus.
- Model the concept/skills as many times as needed to make sure all students are ready to do it on their own.
- Allow many opportunities for students to ask questions and get clarification.

Source: The University of Kansas www.specialconnections.ku.edu/?q=instruction/mathematics/teacher_tools/explicitly_model_mathematics_concepts_skills_and_problem_solving_strategies

Think-Alouds

As mentioned in the steps for planning to use explicit modeling, the teacher should think aloud as you show each step. Think-alouds help the teacher verbalize his or her own thinking, and students are then able to visualize the teacher's thinking. The result is that students learn to think through processes on their own by mimicking the teacher's thought process during the think-aloud. Through the use of think-alouds, students engage in discourse about the important parts of a mathematics problem, the details of a mathematical solution or results of an investigation in science and then express in written or verbal form the decisions they make.

Think-Aloud Mathematics Sample Portion

The Story Problem

Jenna and her brother Sam **weighed** themselves. Jenna weighs 96 and ¼ pounds, and Sam weights 89 and ¼ pounds. How much do they weigh together?

Think-Aloud

First, I make sure that I know **what** the problem is asking me to do.

Then, I look at the last sentence because I see the phrase "how much." That means I need to look for some missing information to complete the problem. I also see the phrase "together," which means I have to add something.

Next, I reread the problem to see what my given information is. I see that the weight of each of person is included. Since the problem asks for weights together, together means all together, and I add.

Finally, I have to add the two fractions. I may need to stop and process here because I need see if the fractions have like denominators. I am comfortable adding with like denominators, so I can continue working the problem. Once I add the two weights, I get 185 and 2/4 pounds.

Modeling a Finished Product

When students are asked to complete a task or assignment, it's important to show them a model of your expectations for a finished product. When asking students to come up with a model (can be a picture or an actual 3D model) of what happens to the water level in a container when you add an object like a rock or lollipop, you might start by showing them exemplary samples of final products other students have developed so they will have some idea of what an original experiment versus a pre-created one looks like. This may be difficult the first time you integrate a new project, as you do not have student samples in your repertoire. For primary students, show them an exemplary example and a "needs work" example or progressing example. However, having a visual example that includes the level of artistic detail and textual evidence you're expecting will help students work at a more rigorous level. In reality, most students do not spontaneously choose to complete their assignments at a high level, so we must show them how to think deeply rather than skimming the surface of an assignment. Don't make them guess what you're looking for; rather, encourage them to take what you've shown them and think of creative, better ways to complete the task. Students' thoughts will become more complex if you set the standard first.

Visual Tools

Our students are visual learners. Our society, as a whole, is becoming more and more reliant on the information we can see, such as infographics, virtual marketing and augmented reality. In order to best reach our students, we must be prepared to make information more visual if the complexity of text is impeding a student's learning process. Using graphics to organize and make sense of written information is a strategy we would hope becomes inherent to each learner.

Anchor Charts

Anchor charts or wall charts are another type of visual tool that can be useful in mathematics and science classrooms. Teachers design anchor charts to provide students with the specific content, strategies, steps, cues or guidelines needed for learning (Miller, 2008 as stated in Armstrong, Ming, and Helf (2018). Anchor charts can also be used for procedural purposes. (See K–5 resource). It is up to you how you create your anchor chart. It should be clearly visible or accessible to all students so that they may use the chart to support their learning.

A useful anchor chart in math relates to prime and composite numbers.

Prime and Composite Numbers

A **prime number** has two factors, 1 and itself . . . ONLY!

A **prime number** has ONLY 1 array.

A **number** such as 7 has a rectangular **array** that looks like this: 1 x 7 or 7 x 1, which means . . .

1. The only factors of 7 are 1 and 7.
2. 7 is a **prime number**.

A **composite number** has more than two factors.

A **composite number** has two or more rectangular arrays.

A **number** such as 15 has two or more rectangular arrays.

1 x 15 and 15 x 1 both = 15

3 x 5 and 5 x 3 both = 15

1. The factors of 15 are 1, 3, 5 and 15, which are more than two factors.
2. 15 is a **composite number**.

In science, you might use a chart when teaching the five senses.

Five Senses	Picture	Types	Examples
See		Color, shape	
Smell		Fruity, sweet, foul (bad)	
Hear		Loud, soft	
Touch		Rough, smooth, soft	
Taste		Sweet, sour, salty	

Graphic Organizers

Graphic organizers are tools with which teachers can help their students organize learning in a way to help them see connections among content, concepts, ideas and facts. Furthermore, the spatial arrangement of a graphic organizer allows the student and the teacher to identify missing information or absent connections in one's strategic thinking (Ellis, 2004). Graphic organizers have been reliable tools for educators for years by helping students make overwhelming information more visual and understandable. Each has its own specific purpose and should be chosen strategically to accomplish the learning goal. What we don't often consider is that you can make your own graphic organizer for any areas in which your students are having trouble thinking at a rigorous level.

Sample Graphic Organizers

Math

Formulas and multiple steps can be challenging for some students. These graphic organizers can be used in mathematics to help guide students through steps to complete a task while allowing students to still do the same work as their classmates.

Sample Reducing a Fraction

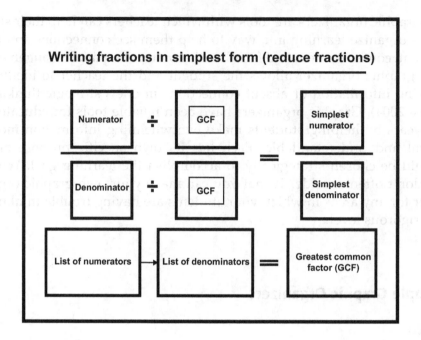

Writing fractions in simplest form (reduce fractions)

| Numerator | ÷ | GCF | | Simplest numerator |
| Denominator | ÷ | GCF | = | Simplest denominator |

List of numerators → List of denominators = Greatest common factor (GCF)

Science

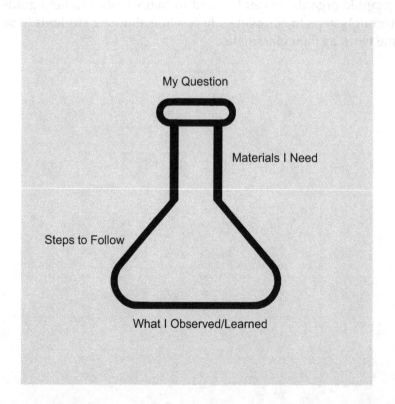

My Question

Materials I Need

Steps to Follow

What I Observed/Learned

If the second graphic organizer looks familiar, it is an adaptation of the Frayer Model for vocabulary. This organizer can be adapted for numerous purposes. In this example, students are studying a topic instead of learning vocabulary, and they can use the organizer to include the important aspects of that topic. Students can complete the organizer in a group setting, or you can do certain parts in a whole group and allow each student to do his own picture and description with vocabulary words that provide some individual practice and demonstration of knowledge. You can also allow students to use words or pictures for any category based on their readiness level.

Venn Diagrams

Venn diagrams are another simple and useful type of graphic organizer that are often used to compare and contrast items or concepts. For example, traditionally your students would compare the differences and similarities of different shapes or compare and contrast mammals and reptiles. To do this traditionally, you would use the example below.

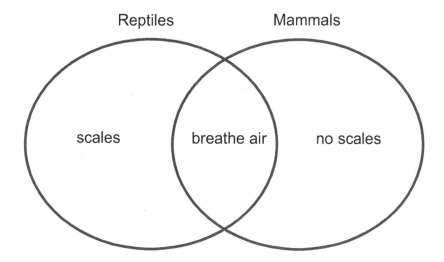

Primary students enjoy completing a physical Venn diagram. Using yarn or string, paper tape and lots of space, create your Venn. Once your physical diagram is ready, give each student in your class a card with a name and symbol or picture of characteristics of mammals and reptiles. For example, students will have cards with words and pictures like scales, no scales, breathes air, lays eggs, gives birth to live offspring, has gills or has lungs. Each student will hold his card up and move to the appropriate space on the Venn diagram. You can do this activity as a preteaching activity, revisit it formatively during the lesson and then use it again after your lesson.

Semantic Feature Analysis

A semantic feature analysis also creates a visual for students trying to synthesize multiple pieces of information. It helps them look for patterns and make connections while acquiring a deeper comprehension of the text.

Sample Semantic Feature Analysis Chart for Shapes in Mathematics					
	Equilateral	Equiangular	Three sides	Four sides	Parallelogram
Rectangle					
Quadrilateral					
Square					
Triangle					

Sample Semantic Feature Analysis Chart for Insects in Science				
	Bites	Lays eggs	Stings	Has Wings
Ants				
Bees				
Lightning bug				
Mosquito				

Foldables

It is effective to provide struggling students with a notes guide or information sheet with extra support to help as they process any new learning. Graphic organizers provide this type of support. A foldable is another example of a graphic organizer that is three dimensional and interactive.

Mathematics Foldable

In mathematics, students can use foldables to help them remember steps or recall vocabulary or concepts. The following foldable is used to help students with mathematics vocabulary that is essential to their knowledge so they can have rich discourse. See more information on discourse in Chapter 5.

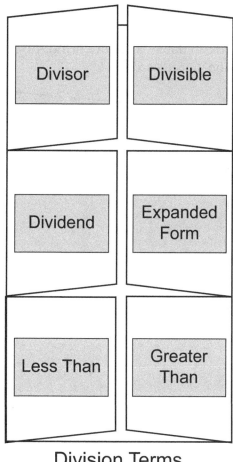

Division Terms

Sample Science Foldable

In the science example, the half fold or book fold is being used to help students recall a new term or concept. Fossil is the term. When you open the half fold, the top half can be used for a definition; the bottom half is used for a picture or example of the word fossil. The back of the half fold can be used for notes, or it may be used for students to summarize a reading on the topic.

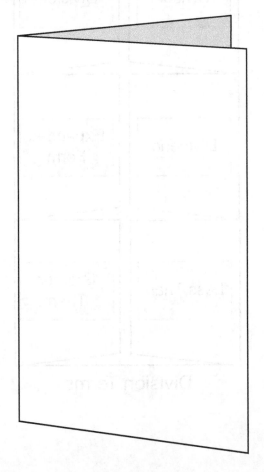

Use the half book foldable vertically or hot-dog style, depending on what your instructional needs are.

Foldables, which can be created traditionally or electronically, have several benefits.

Benefits of Foldables

♦ Organize and graphically represent ideas to help understanding
♦ Clearly see relationships among ideas
♦ Students build ownership of learning since they have choices as to design and inclusion of information.
♦ Require limited resources

Types and Uses

Foldables are very versatile and can be used interchangeably across content areas. However, it is helpful to have a guide as to which types of foldables are best used for the concept you want to use with your students. Dinah Zike provides examples of types of foldables, which gives you a starting point. There are many others; remember, you should customize them to best meet your students' needs. We have given you a starter list of types and ways you can use them, but you will probably want to Google an image so you'll know exactly what each looks like.

Sample Foldables		
Type of Foldable	*Useful For*	*Examples*
Two-Tab Foldable	Lists, definitions and comparison/contrast	Whole numbers and fractions Body parts
Three-Tab or Four-Tab Fold	Sequencing	Steps to complete long division How a flower grows
Accordion Fold	Recording many pieces of information	Story problems along with steps to solve Acids and bases with listed traits and examples

Sample Foldables		
Type of Foldable	*Useful For*	*Examples*
Vocabulary Book	Organizing vocabulary, especially by unit or section	This will work for any mathematics or science content and is appropriate for primary students. They can write, draw pictures or cut out pictures. They can keep a running vocabulary book and be able to take it home at the end to the year to add to it over the summer.

Source: See www.k12.wa.us/IndianEd/TribalSovereignty/High/CWP-HS/Unit4/Level1-Materials/foldables.pdf for picture

Additional Foldables

Foldables have a wide range of uses and are especially helpful for scaffolding learning so that students can learn at higher levels. There are a variety of resources that provide additional information.

Additional Resources

Dinah Zike's Foldables
www.k12.wa.us/IndianEd/TribalSovereignty/High/CWP-HS/Unit4/Level1-Materials/foldables.pdf

Foldable templates and illustrations and ways to use them; general introduction; you'll find pictures of the ones mentioned in the *Sample Foldables* chart in this chapter.

Hands-On Doesn't Mean Minds Off: Using Foldables to Promote Learning: Nancy Frey
www.boostconference.org/workshop_pdf/Hands%20On%20Doesn't%20Mean%20Minds%20Off-Foldables.pdf

Provides context for using foldables and ideas for how to use them in various content areas

Center for Math and Science Education
http://cmase.pbworks.com/w/page/6923144/Foldables

Ideas for math and science foldables

Deepening Understanding

Leading students to a deeper level of learning is at the heart of rigor. However, there are some students who need help to move beyond basic information. Many of the scaffolding techniques mentioned previously help students deepen understanding, but let's discuss some other intentional ways to help them look beyond the surface level of a task or text.

Ways to Help Students Deepen Their Understanding
Concrete-representational-abstract

Flesh it out

Simulations

Reading and writing guides

Concrete-Representational-Abstract

Moving from concrete to abstract thinking in mathematics usually is synonymous with elementary school, but young adolescents also struggle with moving through the phase. Some of their challenge has to do with the development of the brain and the phase of intellectual development they are in, but some of it has to do with instructional practices. It is still an effective practice to support students' learning by using concrete examples and then slowly moving them toward abstract learning. Although this practice is commonly known as a strategy for struggling learners or students who are exceptional or have special needs, it can benefit all students.

Math Sample: Middle and Upper Elementary
Students are first introduced to fractions using concrete objects such as fraction tiles or fraction circles. Students are able to touch the manipulate the objects and touch them so they can identify ½ versus ⅓. Then, the student are shown pictures that represent fractions. Once the student is able to identify the picture, you can move to the abstract phase of learning about fractions. In the abstract phase, students should be able to see a fraction expression and understand it well enough to move on to performing operations with fractions.

Although concrete-representational-abstract (CRA) is a concept usually synonymous with mathematics, the process is a support strategy that can also be used in science. Science is generally hands-on, but there are instances when students are not given concrete examples of what they need to learn, and they struggle to understand later on as they move to the abstract phase of learning. An effective way to use the CRA strategy in the sciences is with topics that are theoretical and conceptually difficult.

Science Sample: Upper Elementary

For convection currents, have students in small groups explore the concept concretely by placing a bottle on their desks, wetting the mouth of the bottle with water and securing a coin on the mouth. Then, they use their hands to warm the bottle so they can observe that heat causes air to escape the bottle. After a robust discussion, which includes trying other adaptations, such as not using water around the mouth of the bottle, students collaborate to create a diagram representing how convection works with air currents (an example other than the bottle). Finally, students individually describe the definition of convection currents, including at least three examples (abstract).

Flesh It Out

Let's look at a fun visual to help students go deeper with a topic. Flesh It Out, originally created by Janet Allen, requires an in-depth analysis of a problem, investigation or historical figure. Rather than simply writing basic information, students are expected to describe more specific information, which allows them to create a finished product with more complexity.

Flesh It Out Math

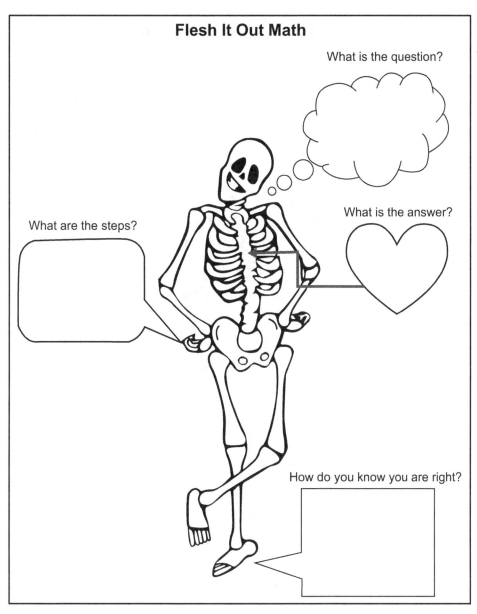

What is the question?

What is the answer?

What are the steps?

How do you know you are right?

In the science classroom, it is a helpful tool to guide students through the process of creating an investigation.

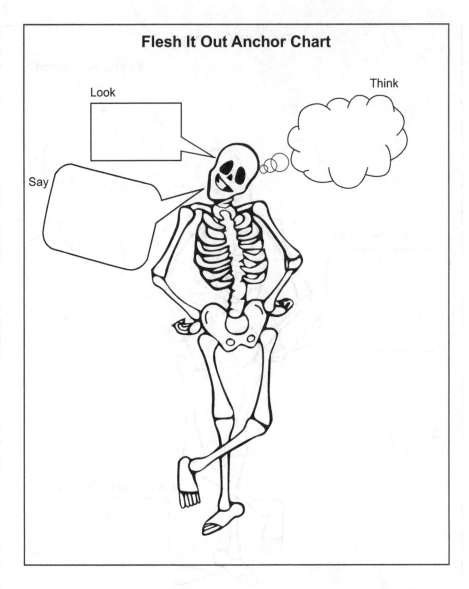

For primary students, *Flesh It Out* can still be used as an anchor chart to guide their mathematical or scientific thinking process. The following adapted version includes three points to consider, but students are still required to use their inquiry skills.

Simulations

Simulations, which require tactile or kinesthetic participation, provide another way for students to be actively engaged in their learning.

Simulations allow students to experience another "world." In other words, they become part of a lab experiment, which allows them to make meaning in a different way, something that is particularly helpful for struggling students. For example, students can use simulations to practice figuring out what their weight on Earth would be on another planet or on the moon, which incorporates mathematics and science content. A variety of web-based resources provide simulations for your students to explore.

Simulations Resources

BrainPOP

www.brainpop.com/

Animated films and simulations for various grade levels. Some resources are free, but your school district must have a license for full services like the use of quizzes.

Gizmos

www.explorelearning.com/

Mathematics and science simulations with an inquiry approach for grades 3 and up. You must sign-up, but it is free.

PhET Interactive Simulations

https://phet.colorado.edu/en/simulations/category/new

Mathematics and science simulations for various topics; particularly strong for mathematics

Molecular Bench

http://mw.concord.org/modeler/

Visual and interactive simulations for science

Simulations and Animations (resource to accompany *The Sourcebook for Teaching Science*)

ww.csun.edu/science/software/simulations/simulations.html

Provides a wide variety of links for science simulations; be aware that some links are inactive

PBS Learning Media

www.pbslearningmedia.org/collection/simulations/

Search by grade and subject to find simulations such as how litter affects our oceans; includes science simulations for elementary grades.

Reading and Writing Guides

Another supportive activity to help you guide students to deeper levels of learning is through the use of reading and writing guides. These tools are effective in providing a road map to problem solving and inquiry in the mathematics and science classroom.

Guide-O-Rama

Students often need assistance with reading text. A Guide-O-Rama guides the students through an assigned text, providing support so they can read and learn at more rigorous levels. Used by students as they read, they are different from regular outlines or study guides in that they take students by the hand and walk them through the text. It's the next best thing to actually sitting down with a student and reading the text with them. The Guide-O-Rama is almost like a think-aloud written down on paper for the student.

How to Build a Guide-O-Rama

1. Identify a chunk of content you need students to read. Guide-O-Ramas should be used with challenging texts that you anticipate students will struggle with.

2. Determine guiding questions that will help them process key portions of the text, similar to what you would use in a traditional study guide.

3. Add think-aloud comments, such as, "Notice that on page 56, there is a box of math or science symbols. When I see a box of text in the margin of the text, I pay special attention since it usually contains important information." These are typically statements and/or questions that you would verbally use to model your thinking for students.

4. Use visuals that will help students remember the content. For example, if students are reading about the Pythagorean theorem, you might put each question in a right triangle.

5. Keep in mind that your goal is twofold: help students process and understand the complex text and move toward independence in learning.

Let's look at excerpts of two Guide-O-Ramas, one for math and one for science. A group of second grade teachers adapted this project by cutting apart the steps of the Guide-O-Rama. As students completed one section, they showed their response to the teacher to receive the next step.

Math Guide-O-Rama		
Chapter 12 Circles Lesson 1		
Page #	Tip	Student Comment
480–481	**Lesson 1 Circles, Radii and Chords** is the title at the top of the page, so automatically I think perhaps I will be learning about parts of the circle. *What are the definitions of radii and chords?* To help me better understand, I am going to look at the box at the top of the page, which includes the words in bold with a definition and a picture.	
482	There are more examples on this page of each of the words mentioned on page 480–481, so I need to identify the words on my own. I can go back and look at the previous pages for help. *Are you able to illustrate an example of radii on your own?* If you answered yes, share your drawing in the space provided. If you can't, write a sentence or two about what you are struggling with.	
483	*List two examples of how radii and chords are used.* This page includes illustrations of radii and chords and prompts me to come up with my own examples of when radii and chords are important in the real world as an option. Although this is an option, I should do it. It will help me later in the unit.	

Guide-O-Ramas also work with nontextbook sources. In this science example, the guide supports students as they read an article from a website on *Air Pollution*.

Science Guide-O-Rama		
Air Pollution		
Section	*Tip*	*Student Comment*
Picture at the top of the page and "What is air pollution?" section	This section is important. I should read the title and the first section to see if this article will help me learn about air pollution: *What can I assume from the title? Do I understand the definition?*	
Natural Causes of Air Pollution and Human Causes of Air Pollution	In these two sections of the article, causes of air pollution are listed. *Did I already know all of these causes? Are there causes that are new to me? In a sentence about natural causes, forest fires are highlighted in blue; this means I should explore this link. It may provide more information about natural causes of pollution.*	
Effects on the Environment	In this section, there is a list with bullets, and after each bullet an effect is listed. *I should read these sections carefully and write a summary for each one.* There are also more words and phrases in blue highlight. *I should explore carbon, carbon cycle and ozone because we talked about these in class. Add these words to my vocabulary notebook.*	
Picture with caption: Smog in the city makes it hard to breathe and see	After seeing the picture after the last section, I realize: *I need to read a little more because this sounds like another effect on the environment. Write about two ways air pollution affects the environment in my own words.*	

Source: From www.ducksters.com/science/environment/air_pollution.php

Another option is a structured writing guide. As with any scaffolding tool or strategy, this writing guide can be adapted to best fit the needs of the student. For upper elementary students, they can work through this strategy alone once you have modeled how to use it with whole or small groups and they have had guided practice time. In math, it guides the student through the process of solving a problem and requires him or her to respond in writing. This process is similar to think-alouds and the Guide-O-Rama in that the students are thinking about the problem and how to solve it, but in this case, you provide a clear step-by-step focus. In a math classroom, you would use this when you are asking students to solve a formula. Personalize your questions. For example, in mathematics you may specifically want the student to do a pictorial representation or model for demonstration of their final solution. You may also be looking for students to use certain skills so you can guide them with your questioning. For example, you can use questioning to guide students toward examining their own reasoning simply by having them stop and ask, "Does this make sense?"

Sample Mathematics Structured Writing Guide

Section 1 Problem Context: Respond to the following questions.
What is the problem asking me to do?
What information am I supposed to be finding?
HINT: Sarah gave Jonathan 12 of her M&M's, and she had 35 left. How many did she have to begin with? Explain how you got your answer. *The problem is asking for the amount of candies Sarah had before she gave some to Jonathan. I also have to explain how I came up with the answer.*

Section 2 Problem-Solving Process: Write the steps you will use to solve the problem.
You should show your work, which means to show every step you used to solve the problem as descriptively as you can. Another person should be able to use your steps to solve the problem with ease. You may use words like "first," "then" or "complete your steps in order as listed."
Step 1 . . .
Step 2 . . .
Step 3 . . .
Step 4 . . .

Sample Mathematics Structured Writing Guide
HINT: First, I read the problem twice to make sure I understood what information I had.
Second, I guessed that Sarah has to have had more than 35 because she has that many after giving some to Jonathan.
Third, since she gave something away, that sounds like take away.
Fourth, I tried to see what I could take 12 away from and get 35, so I guessed. I started with 50 because that is an easy number. I got 38. That's 3 away from the number she had left, so I tried 3 away from 50 and got 47.

Final Section The Solution: Share and justify your answer.
Here you will give your answer and write about how you know your answer is correct by examining your reasoning. Use these prompts to help.
Answer: I got _____ for my answer.
Reasoning: I know it is correct because I _____.
Unacceptable responses for reasoning include but are not limited to:

- ♦ I guessed, and it was right.
- ♦ I asked my partner, and she said it was correct.
- ♦ I looked at it, and it was right.
- ♦ I checked it with the calculator, and it was correct.
- ♦ Every time I did it, I got the same answer, so it must be right.

HINT: I got 47 because it was 3 away from the number I guessed.

I know it's correct because when I add the 12 plus the ones she gave Justin, I got 47.

My friend showed me how I can subtract to get the answer. If she started with 47 and gave

away 12 that is 47−12=35.

In science, you might use the writing guide to assist students in writing a description and analysis of an investigation.

Sample Science Structured Writing Guide

Section 1 Problem Context: Respond to the following questions.
What am I investigating?
Is there a problem I need to solve?
What questions am I to formulate as I move through this investigation?

Section 2 Inquiry or Investigation Process: Write the steps you will follow to explore the investigation
You should describe the process by which you will complete your investigation. For example, you may use the scientific method or similar process. Another person should be able to use your steps to solve the problem with ease. You may use words like "first," "then" or "complete your steps in order as listed."
Step 1 . . .
Step 2 . . .
Step 3 . . .
Step 4 . . .

Final Section Analysis of Your Investigation: Share and support your conclusion.
Here you will share your findings, such as data or found misconceptions, and write about how you know your findings are credible by examining your reasoning. Use these prompts to help.
Answer: I found that _____. OR My results were_____.
Reasoning: I my evidence makes sense because I _____.
Unacceptable responses for reasoning include but are not limited to:
My evidence is credible because my partner confirmed it.
My findings are credible because I followed the scientific method.
I got what everyone else in class got, so my findings are correct.
Every time I did it, I got the same answer, so it must be right.

Toolbox of Strategies

Obviously, we will not be with our students forever, so they must have the tools necessary to be independent thinkers and learners. Our job is to equip them for this by teaching strategies that can eventually be self-selected. The use of instructional strategies allows students to access texts and tasks that may seem too complex at first glance. Teachers are typically well versed in using strategies with our students, but here's where we fall short: We fail to name them with intentionality and explain to our students why we have chosen to use a specific tool to help them. How will they be able to decide which strategy to use on their own if we haven't taught them how to select an appropriate tool to unlock meaning or aid in completion of an assignment?

There are many resources with suggested tools to help students unlock the meaning of texts or work through a challenging writing task in order to integrate strategies into daily learning. The following chart is a sampling of these effective strategies. Again, the goal is to teach students to use the strategies independently when they encounter rigorous material. After using them with intentionality in your classroom, begin to coach students to utilize them on their own by asking them which strategy they think could be applied instead of doing it for them.

Student Strategies		
Strategy	*Definition*	*Purpose*
Chunking the Text	Separating the text into smaller, more manageable sections and setting a purpose for each chunk	To reduce the intimidation factor when encountering long words, sentences or whole texts; to increase comprehension of difficult or challenging text
Marking the Text	Use predetermined markers to interact with the text (i.e., a smiley face for something that excites you, a heart for something you love, a frowny face for text that makes you sad, etc.)	To focus reading for specific purposes and make reading an active process rather than a passive process
Choral Read	Students read a piece of text together or with the teacher.	To increase fluency in reading
Sketching the Text	Students visualize what a scene looks like and sketch it beside the text.	Another way of visualizing, this helps ensure that students are making a movie in their mind as they read.

Student Strategies		
Strategy	*Definition*	*Purpose*
Task Cards	Using cards to outline single, clear tasks to be completed individually, as a group, or at a station	Task cards will keep students focused and create independence during the learning process.
Mapping	Creating a graphic organizer that serves as a visual representation of the organizational plan for a written text	To generate ideas, concepts or key words that provide a focus and/or establish organization during the prewriting, drafting or revision process
Think-Pair-Share	Students are given to time to think about their response to a question before pairing up with a partner to discuss their ideas, and then sharing combined ideas with the larger group.	This strategy allows time for each student to individually process a question and gather thoughts before discussing with others.

Remember, every student will not need every strategy in a given lesson. The beauty of scaffolding is that teachers can choose which strategies to use with a student as they anticipate where they may need assistance or as they notice a learner hitting a roadblock. Familiarity with the strategies will allow you to access them quickly for your students, and their level of comfort with them will allow them to pull them out of their box of tools as needed to access rigorous material in other courses.

Special Populations

We would be remiss to neglect discussing special populations in our classrooms and the scaffolding that can take place to help them access complex tasks. They are not exempt from rigorous activities. When provided with appropriate support, all students can and will be able to complete rigorous activities. Although there are many special groups, we will focus on two: students with special needs and English learners.

Students With Special Needs

Students with special needs do not necessarily have a lower level of intelligence. They are capable of rigorous work, but they need extra support. In addition to the general scaffolding strategies we have discussed, there are additional ways to help them learn.

Core Extensions

Core extensions are designed to extend the learning time of the core content by giving students more time to learn the core curriculum. This approach may allow the student more think time regarding the standard and, if taught correctly, provides the teacher and interventionist the time to enhance the lesson delivery to better meet the needs of the student. For example, use of visuals and concrete manipulative instruction is highly effective for low-performing students. However, these instructional tools require more time for implementation. A core extension allows for that time.

Preteaching

Another option within intervention is to preteach academic content. Many students who receive additional or clarifying instruction on content may start to develop a dependency on that support. If they believe that they are less successful in the core classroom than they are during their support class, then they have the tendency to ignore core instruction and simply wait for the support class to explain what they didn't understand, or worse, didn't try to learn.

Preteaching is when the support or intervention class prepares the students for the upcoming core content instruction. By receiving scaffolding content, the student experiences much of the instruction that he or she will see in the core and can contribute more readily to the conversation in the core. For example, in a lesson on estimating length of objects, the student would begin working on measuring and comparing different objects for accuracy. Next, groups begin practicing their estimation skills. With this preparation, the students would be better prepared for the classroom core instruction. You can follow similar procedures for a science classroom. Preteaching opportunities help students feel more competent and confident in their knowledge. While there is evidence to support preteaching, there are also roadblocks. Much preparation and collaboration with the preteaching interventionist are needed so the content and instructional design best prepare students for success.

Multiple-Meaning Words

Particularly in specific content areas, it's important to teach words that have multiple meanings. A student teacher in a science classroom asked,

"Does anyone know what 'grounded' means?" It was his opening question for a lesson on electricity. Immediately, one student shouted out, "That's what happened to me last week when I made a C on my test!" Everyone laughed, but that's an excellent example of a multiple-meaning word. We need to specifically teach students the different meanings of these words. Janet Allen shares a chart that helps.

Working With Multiple Meaning Words			
Word	In general, this means . . .	In our subject area (math or science), this means . . .	Visual to help me understand
Base	bottom of something, support	The face of a three-dimensional shape	a base
Multiple	many, more than one	Result of one number multiplied by another	3 X 7 = 21 21 is a multiple

Source: www.stenhouse.com/sites/default/files/public/legacy/pdfs/vocabtools.pdf

Keyword Mnemonics

Students with known mathematics disabilities can benefit from the use of mnemonic devices when learning new concepts, information or strategies; however, all students benefit from this type of support (Hott, Isbell, & Montani, 2014) For example, RIDE, a strategy suggested by Mercer, Mercer, and Pullen (2011), is a strategy that provides problem-solving support for students.

RIDE

R—Remember the problem correctly.

I—Identify the relevant information.

D—Determine the operations and unit for expressing the answer.

E—Enter the correct numbers, calculate and check the answer.

The version below is an adapted version you can also do based on what your students need. For example, we chose to use a motorcycle symbol as a visual cue for the problem-solving mnemonic we created.

RIDE

R—Read the problem more than one time.

I— Identify key information.

D—Determine how you need to solve the problem.

E—Examine your solution to see if it makes sense.

You can use this same strategy as an anchor chart for primary students in which you can help them with instructional or noninstructional routines. In the following example, the mnemonic device is used to help students remember the beginning steps to understand how to solve a mathematics problem or how to begin scientific inquiry.

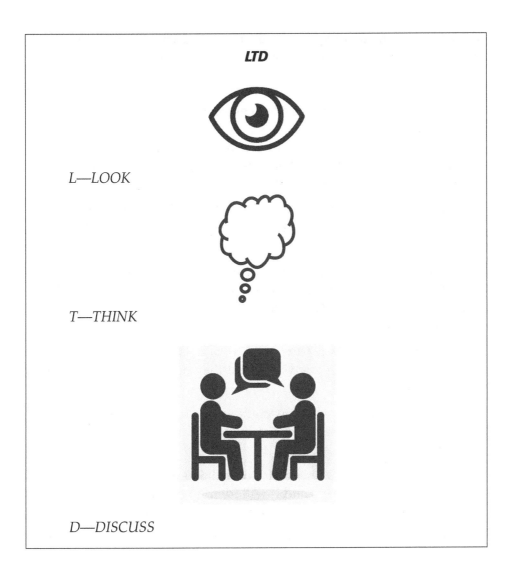

LTD

L—LOOK

T—THINK

D—DISCUSS

Layering Meaning

A particular concern in the science classroom occurs when students cannot read grade-level text. Sometimes you must start with easier text in order to build to more complex text, which will deepen understanding. One strategy for supporting students who are not reading at grade level is "layering meaning." While this strategy can be used for any student who cannot yet read the grade-level or assigned text material, it is particularly helpful for students with special needs because it allows students to read another text on the same topic that is written at an easier level. Students read that selection first to build their own prior knowledge and vocabulary; then they can go back and read the more complex text with your support. It's an excellent strategy—one that encourages rigor because students move beyond the easier text but one that requires texts at differing levels. Technology is our solution. A variety of websites provide leveled texts for your use.

Sources for Leveled Text

News in Levels (www.newsinlevels.com) and **FortheTeachers** (www.fortheteachers.org/reading_skills/) provide varying levels of an article or text. FortheTeachers has science, health and other topics, but information is language arts oriented.

Books That Grow (www.booksthatgrow.com) has a library of texts that have each been edited to be made accessible to different reading levels. There is a fee.

TweenTribune (http://tweentribune.com) is produced by the Smithsonian. It also provides an article at different levels but adds a quiz (moderately high-level questions) and allows teachers to create virtual classrooms to monitor progress and moderate comments.

Readworks (www.readworks.org) is a little different—the site offers texts, including paired texts, but they do *not* provide differing levels of the same text.

Text Compactor (www.textcompactor.com) lets you paste text into it and then automatically summarizes it (with a customized setting you control).

Rewordify (http://rewordify.com) allows a teacher or student to paste text into the screen, and it will identify challenging words and replace them with simpler ones or with explanations.

Freckle (freckle.com) provides an online reading platform, with a preassessment tool, that students can use to read texts at various levels.

Thanks to Larry Ferlazzo for these sources.

English Learners

English learners also have unique needs, some of which are met by the general scaffolding strategies we discussed. However, there are also more customized strategies that are helpful.

Technology

English learners are often given simplified activities due to the language barrier. However, their lack of knowledge in speaking or writing

English does not mean their growth in math, science or other subjects should be stifled. Technology offers a wide array of constantly evolving tools to support students who learn differently. Discovery Education online allows students the opportunity to read, watch and learn in their native language while they are learning English. Google Translate can take any text and convert it to one of 300 languages so that students can still access the content and learn at a high level. Likewise, students with a learning disability in writing can use Screencasting, Nearpod or Flip-Grid, which allow students to record themselves on any device, explaining their answer to a prompt or understanding of a text. Remember, the answers don't always have to come in the form of writing! Students who struggle with reading could use Microsoft Learning tools as a platform to break texts apart or have them read aloud to build fluency, confidence and comprehension; Newsela and Freckle offer reading platforms that provide options for teachers to assign the same text with the same content but at various Lexile levels. All of these free tools will allow your special population to still have access to rigorous thinking and problem solving.

Visual Coding

Using color to deconstruct or draw attention to parts of a text can help English learners process information more effectively. This can be done by the teacher or by the student as you gradually release independence. When reading an article or a piece of text on static electricity, students can underline in purple what it means (definition) and underline in green what causes static electricity. Additionally, if students were reading about other types of electricity, they could underline or highlight how those different types of electricity work in comparison or contract to static electricity. For example, they may outline or highlight how circuits work for lights to be switched on and off. Highlighting is particularly helpful to allow students to highlight key information they will need. If a teacher is consistent throughout the year with the same visual coding practices, students will recognize patterns more readily. For example, when showing examples of how to multiply two-digit by two-digit numbers, always highlight the ones product in the same colors, highlight the tens in a different color and circle what is added to the tens. Finally underline the final answer. This will assist students as they peer edit each other's work because they can use the same text markings to identify correct steps or missing steps.

Three-Column Note Taking

Oftentimes, students are simply asked to take notes, and they write down either everything in the text or nothing. They do the same with teacher lectures. We've found that English learners take the best notes when they are provided with structure. Many teachers use a simple, two-column note-taking form. Key words are written in the left column. Using those as prompts, students take notes in the right column, with an appropriate numbering system provided so students know the exact amount of information to write. You can also add a third column, providing a place for students to draw an image that would remind them of the information.

Three-Column Note Taking		
Key Words (Provided)	Students' Notes	Reminder Drawing

Other Strategies

There are a variety of other strategies you can use with your English learners. Remember to choose the one(s) that best meet(s) your students' needs.

Other Strategies

♦ Provide opportunities to participate in small groups or work with a partner.

♦ Respect that they may need more reflection time, so you will need to provide more wait time.

♦ Allow some use of native language during scaffolding time.

♦ Be aware of cultural examples or vocabulary students may be unaware of.

♦ Allow for *Show and Tell*. This fosters safety and motivation in that the student gets an opportunity to share something he or she is interested in.

Conclusion

Supporting your students so they are able to access rigorous material and learn at high levels is crucial. The majority of your students will not intuitively or voluntarily think on a critical level unless you lead them to that point. This does not mean they are not capable. It simply means they need to be taught *how* to learn challenging material by providing them with tools to unlock meaning as well as receiving ongoing prompting to stimulate deeper thinking. As you increase the level of rigor for students, you will need to increase your support and scaffolding.

Points to Ponder

- The most important thing learned . . .
- One strategy I want to implement now . . .
- One strategy I want to save for later . . .
- I'd like to learn more about . . .
- I'd like to share with other teachers . . .

5

Demonstration of Learning

In Chapter 3, we discussed rigorous expectations, including providing examples of rigorous tasks and assignments. In this chapter, we provide a variety of classroom approaches that allow students to demonstrate their understanding at a deeper level.

Five Areas
1. Rigorous questioning strategies
2. Inquiry-based instruction
3. Academic discourse
4. Examining reasoning
5. Think like a mathematician/scientist

Rigorous Questioning Strategies

Our questioning strategies reflect our high expectations. When we ask students higher-order questions, we are showing them we expect them to answer at higher levels. On the other hand, when we only ask students recall questions such as, "Who did this?" we are demonstrating that we don't really expect them to know any more than the most basic answers. There are several general strategies you should incorporate as you question students.

General Questioning Strategies

♦ Provide adequate wait time.

♦ Call on a variety of students, not just those who raise their hands.

♦ Ask higher-order questions.

♦ If you ask a lower-level question, follow up with a higher-order question.

♦ Encourage follow-up questions from students.

♦ If a student struggles with the answer, provide guidance and scaffolding rather than moving to another student.

Note: Some researchers identify two types of wait time. Wait time type I, which may be lengthy, occurs between teachers' questions and teachers' reactions and between teachers' actions and students' responses. In wait time II, teachers give feedback to the students, which is typically immediate.

Types of Questioning

Next, we'll look at four models for rigorous questioning. Each provides insight into effective questioning. Choose or blend models to help you craft rigorous questioning for your lesson.

Four Questioning Models

1. Four categories

2. Transfer of learning

3. Essential questions

4. Objective-based questioning

Four Categories

Another way to look at questioning is a set of four categories developed by James Gallagher and Mary Jane Aschner (1963). These blend nicely with Webb's Depth of Knowledge levels that we discussed earlier.

Four Categories

1. Memory questions focus on identifying, naming, defining, designating and responding with yes or no. Key words are who, what, where and when.

2. Convergent-thinking questions focus on explaining, stating relationships, comparing and contrasting. Key words are why, how, and in what way.

3. Divergent-thinking questions focus on predicting, hypothesizing, inferring and reconstructing. Key words are imagine, suppose, predict, if . . . then . . ., how might, can you create and what are some possible consequences.

4. Evaluative-thinking questions focus on valuing, defending, judging and justifying choices. Key words are defend, judge, justify, what do you think and what is your opinion.

Transfer of Learning

In their book, *Tools for Teaching Conceptual Understanding*, Julie Stern and Krista Ferraro discuss transfer of learning. Based on earlier work by Perkins and Saloman, they focus specifically on students' transfer of learning. They distinguish the transfer as academic or real world and high road (more rigorous) or low road (less rigorous).

Stern and Ferraro's Transfer of Learning		
Transfer to Academic Learning	Low Road (less rigorous)	Transfer to highly similar school tasks
Transfer to Academic Learning	High Road (more rigorous)	Transfer to highly dissimilar school tasks
Transfer to Real-World Learning	Low Road (less rigorous)	Transfer to highly similar, real-world scenarios
Transfer to Real-World Learning	High Road (more rigorous)	Transfer to highly dissimilar, real-world scenarios (innovation)

Let's look at how this works in the mathematics and science classrooms.

Math Examples

Type of Transfer	Low Road	High Road
Academic	Compute the answer for 359 ÷ 6	How can you use your knowledge of long division to figure out how much money each of your classmates will receive to spend at the souvenir shop if your class raised a certain amount of money?
Real World	What is a real-life example of a problem in which you would use long division?	Your grandmother won $1000, and she decided to split it with her 8 grandchildren. How much money would each of you, each grandchild, receive? Show various ways you can figure out the answer.

Science Examples

Type of Transfer	Low Road	High Road
Academic	How did the information on the water cycle relate to what you know about cloud formation?	Next year, we will be studying changes in the Earth's land. How do you think our unit on landforms will prepare us for that content?
Real World	How does the water cycle relate to us when it rains?	How does a drought or a flood affect the water cycle?

For primary students, the process is the same, but your students might verbalize their responses.

Essential Questions

Another way to look at questioning is through the seven defining characteristics of essential questions. Jay McTighe and Grant Wiggins (2013) explain: "[A]im is to stimulate thought, to provoke inquiry, and to spark more questions including thoughtful student questions, not just page answers. They are provocative and generative. By tackling such questions, learners are engaged in uncovering the depth and richness of a topic that might otherwise be obscured by simply covering it (p. 3)."

Seven Defining Characteristics of Essential Questions

1. Open ended
2. Thought provoking and intellectually engaging
3. Calls for higher-order thinking
4. Points toward important, transferable ideas
5. Raises additional questions
6. Requires support and justification
7. Recurs over time

Sample Essential Questions	
Math	*Science*
◆ When and why should we estimate? ◆ Is there a pattern? ◆ How does *what* we measure influence *how* we measure? How does *how* we measure influence *what* we measure (or don't measure)? ◆ What do good problem solvers do, especially when they get stuck? ◆ How accurate (precise) does this solution need to be? ◆ What are the limits of this math model and of mathematical modeling in general?	◆ What makes objects move the way they do? ◆ How are structure and function related in living things? ◆ Why and how do scientific theories change? ◆ How can we best measure what we cannot directly see? ◆ How do we decide what to believe about a scientific claim?

Objective-Based Questioning

Faculty at Washington University organize open-ended questions around twelve objectives. Consider how these apply to mathematics and science. It is important that you think about the readiness level or academic ability level of your students and if any adjustments are necessary.

Objective-Based Questions for Science	
Objective	*Description*
To assess learning	◆ What is the most important idea that was generated in today's discussion? ◆ Write, draw or explain how your learning relates to real life.
To ask a student to clarify a vague comment	◆ Elaborate on the point you made about sound waves. ◆ Explain what you mean when you say sound waves affect objects.
To prompt students to explore attitudes, values or feelings (when appropriate)	◆ What are the beliefs the scientist uses to share his opinion on a controversial issue in science? Example: global warming ◆ What is your initial reaction to this argument?
To prompt students to see a concept from another perspective	◆ How do you think this issue is viewed by those with whom you disagree? ◆ How does that concept apply to this new problem?
To ask a student to refine a statement or idea	◆ How could you explain your answer differently? ◆ How can you narrow your research question?
To direct students to respond to one another	◆ What do you think about the idea just presented by your classmate? ◆ Do you agree, or do you see the issue differently? Explain. ◆ Can you think of another way to solve that problem?

Objective-Based Questions for Math	
Objective	*Description*
To prompt students to investigate a thought process	◆ What are the assumptions that informed the design of this experiment? ◆ What assumptions is your reasoning built on in the mathematical proof?
To ask students to predict possible outcomes	◆ What might happen if you used XXX strategy to solve the problem? ◆ Would you get a different result?
To prompt students to connect and organize information	◆ How does this article explain more about what we studied last week? ◆ Can you develop a graph or table that organizes this information in a helpful way?
To ask students to apply a principle or formula	◆ How does this principle apply to the science investigation you completed? ◆ Who can suggest how we might use this new formula to solve the problems we examined at the start of class today? ◆ When is your solution not valid or does not make sense?
To ask students to illustrate a concept with an example	◆ Can you think of another real-life example of what happened during your experiment? How does your research support your example? ◆ Can you point us to a specific part of the problem that led you to that conclusion? ◆ Can you identify a table, graph or design that exemplifies that idea?
To prompt students to support their assertions and interpretations	◆ How do you know that? ◆ Which part of the text led you to that conclusion?

Source: Adapted from: http://teachingcenter.wustl.edu/resources/teaching-methods/participation/askingquestions-to-improve-learning/

You may want to use technology to support your questioning efforts. There are a variety of apps that can enhance your instruction.

Apps to Use With Questioning

AnswerGarden—A tool for online brainstorming or polling, educators can use this real-time tool to see student feedback on questions.

Animoto—Gives students the ability to make a short, thirty-second share video of what they learned in a given lesson

Answer Pad—A graphical student response system with the ability to poll and leave feedback. The blank pad functions like an individual whiteboard for each student.

AudioNote—A combination of a voice recorder and notepad that captures both audio and notes for student collaboration

Dotstorming—A whiteboard app that allows digital sticky notes to be posted and voted on. This tool is best for generating class discussion and brainstorming on different topics and questions.

Obsurvey—Create surveys, polls and questionnaires quickly and easily

PollDaddy—Quick and easy way to create online polls, quizzes and questions. Students can use smartphones, tablets and computers to provide their answers, and information can be culled for reports.

Poll Everywhere—Teachers can create a feedback poll or ask questions. Students respond in various ways, and teachers see the results in real time. With open-ended questions, you can capture data and spin up tag clouds to aggregate response. There is a limit to the number of users.

The Queue—Free educational chat tool that mirrors Twitter and allows teachers to post questions and students to respond via the thread. Students can respond via text or video, and the tool allows "journeys" in which teachers introduce a topic via video and connect students to participating resources. Great for gathering formative assessment data at the beginning, middle or end of units.

Source: www.nwea.org/blog/2018/the-ultimate-list-65-digital-tools-and-apps-to-support-formative-assessment-practices/

Inquiry-Based Instruction

Although inquiry is usually equated with science, inquiry is also essential in mathematics. Use of inquiry in mathematics helps students become mathematical thinkers, just as its use in science encourages students to process information from a scientific perspective. The idea of inquiry in mathematics and science is to move students away from a traditional way of learning. In inquiry-based learning in mathematics, students are not finding a missing value in a mathematics sentence or finding the area of a perfect square by counting square blocks. Instead of looking for one value, a student may be given various values with which they are required to find real-life connections. This is a teacher model, but you may also incorporate a simplified version for students to use in small groups. Primary students are naturally curious; these steps can help you structure that curiosity.

Inquiry-Based Instruction	
Math	*Science*
1. "Inquiry-based teaching prioritizes process over product." 2. Investigation is at the core of inquiry-based teaching. Students investigate an issue or problem to find an answer. 3. Collaborative groupings are encouraged. "Students assist one another throughout the learning process, which enables them to share and build upon ideas as well as articulate how they arrived at a solution." 4. Teachers serve as facilitator ONLY and co-investigator only. "As the students work together, the teacher can move from group to group, listening to their discussions. Teachers may ask questions to gauge students' understanding and correct any misconceptions." 5. "Students solve math problems that have a meaningful life application." You must design a structure that is stable in the event of an earthquake. How will your knowledge of geometry aid in this process?	Inquiry Cycle 1. Inquisition: Start with a question to investigate 2. Acquisition: Brainstorming possible solutions. 3. Supposition: Selecting a statement to test 4. Implementation: Designing and carrying out a plan 5. Summation: Collecting evidence and drawing conclusions 6. Exhibition: Communicating and sharing results

Source: Math information from: https://academicpartnerships.uta.edu/articles/education/inquiry-based-learning-math-classroom.aspx (some portions adapted)

Science Cycle from: from Llewellyn (2013), *The inquiry cycle*

Becoming an Inquiry-Based Teacher

According to Llewellyn (2013), there are five necessary steps to becoming an inquiry-based teacher. Although originally designed for the science classroom, the steps are adaptable for the math classroom.

Steps to Become an Inquiry-Based Teacher

1. "Build an understanding of inquiry"—Science is based on investigations, which start with questions, and it does not always occur in a step-by-step process like with the scientific method.

2. "Develop and understanding of the change process"—In other words, change will not happen immediately; moving from a classroom with more transitional practices to inquiry-based practices will take time.

3. "Construct a mindset for emerging pedagogy"—Accepting the idea and reality that students move beyond only gaining knowledge from what we give them but can construct their own knowledge.

4. "Translate new knowledge into practice"—Seek ways to translate current labs into more inquiry-based labs and learn how to "enhance your questioning skills." "Inquiry is not just finding the right answers; it's seeking the right questions."

5. "Create a culture of inquiry" with an overall emphasis on questioning (pp. 60–61).

Integrated Lesson

Introduction: Collect and display a variety of shaped containers. Have the students list the containers in order, least to greatest based on their estimate of the volume of each, in their math journal. Ask students to share their ideas, thoughts and methods for determining the container with the greatest volume. Ask students what volume is. What did they look at? Is the height more important than the width or circumference? Where do they see a volume measurement in real life? How do we measure volume? Share with students which containers are larger than others with a quick measurement of the volume of several of the containers.

Procedures in Summary: Students use different materials or items to determine volume such as rice, lentils and water. Students explore their knowledge of mass and volume to determine which item provides the best estimate for volume.

Probing Questions: Ask students to compare the relationship between different solids. Do they see any relationships? If students can see a similarity, have them share and discuss their findings. If they cannot see a relationship, aim them toward the cube and square pyramid. Was their measurement of the square pyramid 1/3 of the cube? What are some ways in which they can prove their findings to be true? Can they see any other similarities with other shapes?

Source: See www.uen.org/lessonplan/view/18993 for complete lesson plan including family connections and suggestions for special populations

Primary Example

Two scientists have mixed up two materials. They know one is seeds and one is eggs, but they have no idea which is which. How can we help them solve that problem?

Source: Example shared by Lindsay Ball on www.edutopia.org/practice/inquiry-based-learning-teacher-guided-student-driven

Through the inquiry process, students are prompted to think through and explain the process rather than simply suppling an answer. They also require students to engage in problems beyond the text with real-life connections.

There are a variety of sources for more information.

Inquiry-Based Learning Resources for Mathematics and Science

Galileo.org Educational Network
http://galileo.org/classroom-examples/
Inquiry-based lesson plan ideas

Lesson Plans and Action Research
https://21cif.com/resources/lessondb/
Extensive lesson plan database with lessons of varying levels of rigor

National Science Digital Library and NSF
http://expertvoices.nsdl.org/middle-school-math-science/
You can pull information by content area or by standard (Common Core Mathematics or Next Generation Science).

Concept to Classroom
www.thirteen.org/edonline/concept2class/inquiry/demo_sub1.html
Inquiry-based workshop for mathematics and science and www.thirteen.org/edonline/concept2class/inquiry/demonstration.html

Videos of inquiry-based lessons

National Council of Teachers of Mathematics
http://illuminations.nctm.org

NCTM Illuminations site

National Science Foundation
www.nsf.gov/news/classroom/people.jsp Lesson plans for various
   content topics

AAAS Science NetLinks http://sciencenetlinks.com/lessons/

Search lesson plans by grade and theme (chemistry, physics, etc.)

Discovery Education
www.discoveryeducation.com/teachers/free-lesson-plans/scientific-
   inquiry-episodel.cfm Teacher resources and inquiry-based lesson plans

Succeeding With Inquiry in Science and Math Classrooms (Jeff C. Marshall)
A book to help guide inquiry-based lesson plans and activities
Teaching High School Science Inquiry and Argumentation (Douglas Llewellyn)

Shares a framework for inquiry and sample ideas, strategies and projects

Rigorous Conversations: Academic Discourse

Academic discourse is critical to learning in all subject areas. In a science classroom, students discussing instructional concepts using academic vocabulary enhances student learning. Effective mathematics discourse or mathematical conversations not only enhances a student's mathematical learning; it also helps them learn how to interact with and communicate with others, which is a skill they will use in everyday life (Sammons, 2018).

When we think about traditional student talk, whether it is in response to a teacher's question, discussion with other students or generating questions, there are common problems.

Problems With Student Talk in the Classroom
- ◆ Controlled by teacher
- ◆ Too little student talk
- ◆ Too focused on simply answering teacher's questions
- ◆ Surface level rather than in depth
- ◆ Dominated by a few students, typically excluding struggling students

---

In recent years, the conversation has shifted from classroom talk and discussion to student discourse, which is also called accountable talk. What exactly is the difference? Student discourse is focused on "on-task" talk, as well as the use of academic vocabulary. In other words, not only is discourse more rigorous; it is also more purposeful.

PURPOSEful Discourse

Promotes critical thinking

Understanding at a deep level is desired result

Reflection is encouraged

Partners, group and individuals use academic vocabulary

Ownership by students

Specific classroom norms enable discourse

Each student participates

Fully implemented as a natural part of the classroom

User-friendly environment facilitates participation by all

Leadership shared with students

Promotes Critical Thinking

Simple, low-level conversations should be, at best, a minor part of your classroom. Although there is a time and place for basic information, discourse should always lead to higher-level, critical thinking.

Sample Prompting Tasks		
	Low Level	*Critical Thinking*
Math	Provide a basic problem to solve.	When provided a problem that was solved using three strategies, students determine which strategy is the most efficient and explain why.
Science	Provide a step-by-step lab to complete.	After students research scientific evidence around a particular topic, they develop a line of inquiry that could be investigated.

For example, Abbigail's son Justin thought that 10 plus 6 is 106. When Abbigail explained that to add 10 + 6 means that you have 10 ones plus 6 more ones, he suddenly yelled "It's 16, Mommy!" When she asked how he added so quickly, he stated, "I used base ten and added 6." Although Abbigail and her son had a lower-level conversation, there are indications that her six-year old son is capable of higher-level thinking. Either Abbigail or his teacher could have probed Justin for more information to determine his exact level of understanding.

STEM Activity
Growing Crops for a Lunar Biosphere
Students collaboratively choose two plants to monitor in classroom biospheres over a period to four weeks to collect data. Once groups have collected and shared data, they will use that information to create their own lunar biosphere in which all class plans would be able to survive.

Skills Incorporated: Use of Discourse and Collaboration, Engineering Process
Discourse and collaboration context: In this project, students will be working together as a team of engineers, mathematicians and scientists. It's imperative that they are able to understand content-specific discourse. For example, they will be using units of measure in mathematical vocabulary like centimeters or inches as well as comparison words such as increase, same as, etc. They will need to be able to use tools like a ruler. They will also need to use scientific vocabulary like humidity, atmosphere and environment, and they will need to use tools like a thermometer. Collaboration will be essential during this project because there are various roles for students to consider; they can choose roles, or you may assign roles that support their strengths.

Source: From: *Stem by design: Strategies and activities for grades 4–8* (2017)

Understanding at a Deep Level Is Desired Result

Similar to promoting critical thinking, discourse results in deeper understanding.

Examples of Discourse That Lead to Deeper Understanding	
Math	*Science*
◆ Offering possible solutions to a problem ◆ Discussion of other applications of a concept ◆ Discussion of relationship of a concept to other concepts	◆ Discussion of possible research questions ◆ Developing a hypothesis or speculating as to a solution ◆ Thorough discussion of results and implications of an investigation

Reflection Is Encouraged

Reflection should be an ongoing part of discourse. Students should self-reflect, which then results in partner or group reflection. Students may need starter prompts to guide the reflective process.

Sample Reflection Prompts (Sample Self-Reflection in Parentheses)

◆ Why do you think . . .? (I wonder why . . .?)
◆ How did you decide . . . ? (I did this because . . . ?)
◆ Have you considered . . . ? (What if I . . . ?)
◆ What would you suggest for . . . ?
◆ How might a mathematician . . . ?
◆ What was your intention when . . . ?
◆ What is the connection between _____ and _____?
◆ What criteria did you use to . . . ? (What criteria did I use to . . . ?)
◆ How would a scientist . . . ?

Partners, Groups and Individuals Use Academic Vocabulary

A key distinguishing mark of discourse is the use of academic language. You'll want to incorporate academic vocabulary throughout your instruction and model its use so students will use it in their discussions.

Sample Academic Vocabulary	
Math	Science
Add	Acid
Balance	Atom
Cube	Base
Dividend	Convection
Divisor	Environment
Estimate	Gas
Equation	Humidity
Factor	Mass
Pattern	Predict
Volume	Thermometer

Ownership by Students

We discussed the importance of developing student ownership in Chapter 2, but we'd like to reinforce that in this context. Academic discourse is more effective when students share ownership. You can facilitate ownership by providing choices in how they discuss content or giving them a voice in the development of the structure of groups. For example, you may allow students to choose their groups, although you need to be careful about students excluding others or cliques that may develop. You might also introduce the lesson and allow students to decide appropriate times to work in pairs or small groups.

Specific Classroom Norms Enable Discourse

If we want to incorporate discourse into our classroom, we cannot assume that it will automatically occur. In addition to teaching students what to discuss, we need to provide and teach a set of norms explaining how to discuss. For primary students, choose three to four norms that are easy to remember and post them with pictures or symbols for visual cues. For example, *Listen to Everyone*, *Wait Your Turn*, *Mistakes Are Okay*.

Sample Classroom Norms for Discourse

- ◆ We are all a team, so we work together rather than competing.
- ◆ We respect each other and act appropriately.
- ◆ We actively listen to each other, which allows us to authentically contribute our perspectives.
- ◆ If you don't agree with someone, find a positive way to respond without embarrassing the other person.
- ◆ Everyone should be able to participate. If one person is talking too much, the other group members should give them a signal and move on.
- ◆ The process is just as important as the result. We want to think deeply about our work, elaborate, justify our points and pose additional questions to promote more thinking.
- ◆ Making mistakes is normal; it helps us learn.
- ◆ If you need help, check out the Resource Board for questioning prompts and/or sample vocabulary.

Each Student Participates

As we said earlier, a challenge you likely face is when a few students dominate discussions, whether it is in the whole class or in small groups or pairs. When you are guiding a whole-class discussion, you can minimize this by calling on a variety of students, regardless of who volunteers. You can also provide an opportunity to share with a partner before you ask for answers as a whole group, which encourages participation. In small groups, if you have issues with particular students and an individual conversation does not take care of the issue, you might consider using a timer or a timekeeper to limit the amount of time each student can speak or using tokens to be used for each comment. When a student runs out of tokens, they are no longer allowed to speak. Although neither of these is ideal since they inhibit conversation, it may be necessary to ensure all students can participate.

A related challenge to participation is when students get stuck or don't know what to say, and therefore they don't say anything. In this case, we want to encourage students, which we can do by providing question starters. The goal is for other students to ask the starter questions so that the group can continue its discussion.

Starter Questions

To Prompt More Thinking:
- You are on the right track. Tell us more.
- You are onto something. Keep going.
- The teacher said there is not right answer, so what would be your best answer?

To Fortify or Justify a Response
- What is your opinion about . . . ?
- Why is what you said important?
- Explain how you got that answer.

To See Others' Points of View
- How is your process different from mine?
- Do you see another way we could come up with a solution?

To Consider Consequences
- How can we apply this to real life?
- What did you learn in another lesson that we can connect this to?
- How else can we use this?

Source: Adapted From: http://ptgmedia.pearsoncmg.com/images/9780205627585/downloads/Echevarria_math_Ch1_TheAcademicLanguageofMathematics.pdf

Fully Implemented as a Natural Part of the Classroom

Discourse is most effective when it is a regular, expected part of the classroom. There are two common ways to incorporate discourse. First, students can respond to our questions, which is an important aspect of the classroom but one that should not overshadow other opportunities. Ideally, you provide options for students to share with each other through pair-share or other options before they share out in the whole group.

Next, students can work collaboratively in small groups. This is a common activity, but for us to provide a more rigorous experience, we must focus what students are doing to encourage higher-order thinking.

Stations and Collaboration

Work stations are intended for the individual or groups of students to practice skills with a specific purpose (Newton, 2018). They can be used to introduce a skill, practice a skill or for the teacher to provide enrichment. Opportunities for discourse can also be provided while students participate in center or station activities.

Sample Station Activities

Math Example: Dividing fractions **Station 1:** Students explore situations in which dividing fractions occur in everyday life **Station 2:** Students practice dividing fractions with concrete models (this station and station 1 do not have to occur in order) **Station 3:** Students use graphic organizers to guide them through the process of dividing fractions (explicit instruction within a center, this can be the station in which the teacher is present for individualized instruction). **Station 4:** Students connect to prior learning from stations 1 and 2 and solve story problems in which they have to divide fractions.	*Science Example: Adaptations and natural selections among different species or animals* **Station 1:** Students brainstorm a list individually about what they know and then combine the list as a group. **Station 2:** Students are introduced to the topic by reviewing key points from a class presentation, or they read an article and summarize key points as part of an interactive reading guide; they could also refer back to brainstorm lists and make changes. **Station 3:** Students choose an animal and discuss adaptations that may occur by 2035 so the animal can survive on Earth. Students will have to take into consideration changes expected by then.

> *Primary Example: Adding*
> **Station 1:** Students use concrete models to practice addition.
> **Station 2:** Student use an interactive tool like a simulation or video on BrainPOP to practice adding. Stations 1 and 2 can happen simultaneously.
> **Station 3:** Students create their own story problems with addition.

User-Friendly Environment Facilitates Participation by All

A variety of factors facilitate an environment in which all students are willing to and even want to participate. We've already talked about minimizing those students who dominate discussions and building ownership by allowing for choice and voice. However, we also need to consider that students are more willing to participate when they feel it is safe to do so. As we discussed in Chapter 2, there are three ways to help students feel safe and secure. These are particularly important as students participate in discourse.

Helping Students Feel Safe and Secure
+ Provide risk-free opportunities to learn.
+ Encourage students to take risks.
+ Teach students to learn from mistakes.

Additionally, you can use technology that facilitates participation. We've found there are times that technology encourages more participation, especially from students who need time for reflection or who are reluctant to speak up in a group.

Technology Resources for Academic Discourse	
Backchannel Chat Price: $15/year/ class; $299/ year/ school **Platforms:** Android, Chrome, iOS and web **Grades:** 7–12	Backchannel Chat's moderated online discussions are intended to engage students and encourage them to share. Think of it as a teacher-moderated, private version of Twitter where students can discuss topics that might just transcend the virtual space. Setup is quick and easy: Teachers sign up, name their chat and give students the URL. Students can join with only a name; no other personal information is required. Teachers can moderate discussions, remove messages and "lock" the chat at any time.
NowComment **Price:** Free **Platforms:** Web **Grades:** K–12	NowComment is a document-annotation and discussion platform that allows students to mark up and discuss texts. Upload a document (in any number of formats) to create an online discussion area. Paragraphs for text are numbered, with the document shown on the left and the comment panel on the right. You can control when students can comment on a document and when they can see each other's comments. For group projects or peer-reviewed activities, you can have students upload their own documents.
Chalkup **Price:** Free for teachers; school/district pricing varies **Platforms:** Android, Chrome, iOS and web **Grades:** 6–12	First and foremost, Chalkup is an LMS (learning management system). However, what makes Chalkup unique among LMSs is that all of its features are framed around discussion and collaboration. Beyond discussions, the platform—like many LMSs—is great for online assignments and grading. If you also happen to be looking for an LMS for your class, Chalkup could be a good way to go.

Leadership Shared With Students

Finally, we want to encourage discourse by providing specific opportunities for students to take on leadership roles in their groups. See a sample of roles you may choose to assign to your students or allow them to choose from.

Sample Roles Within Math and Science Groups
- Project manager
- Group leader
- Developer
- Recorder
- Fact checker
- Presenter or spokesperson
- Materials manager
- Researcher
- Data collector
- Data analyzer

Examining Reasoning

Students should not only be able to think critically and reason when they are trying to solve a problem or discover a solution to a problem; they should be able to examine their own reasoning and the reasoning of others to make sure their decisions are credible. This includes analyzing information for errors, analyzing errors themselves and stating a claim and supporting it with appropriate evidence. Examining reasoning should occur on a regular basis so that students hone those skills. Also, students should use appropriate math or science vocabulary. There are specific applications for both math and science classrooms.

Examples	
Math Examples	*Science Examples*
◆ Given one or more solved problems, determine and explain any errors and correct them. Justify your corrections. ◆ Assess options for solving a problem and choose the most efficient. Justify your choice. ◆ Explain and justify an alternate way to prove a mathematical conclusion.	◆ Describe errors (particularly data errors) given the results in a science investigation. ◆ Explain the most efficient way to determine the accuracy of a hypothesis. ◆ Assess a scientist's claim about an issue. Determine if it is supported by evidence and through applications in real life. ◆ Example: After watching a video of a debate on an issue, discuss the various perspectives. Then, working in groups, choose another issue, research the varying perspectives and debate that issue.

STEM Example
The Science Behind Working Out

Students will work as a group to a create a boat made of rocks that will float and carry a small piece of fruit to mimic a person. First, students will decide if a rock will float or not. Then, they will test various rocks to see which has the best floating capacity. Once this happens, they will design their rock boat. During the process, students will convey their reasoning for the rock they chose. Prompts. We chose this rock because . . .? It make since because when we . . . we figured out. . . . Our fruit floated or did not float because . . . Now we should . . .

Skills incorporated: creating viable arguments and examining one's own reasoning, as well as the reasoning of others

Source: Adapted from *Teaching STEM in the early years: Activities for integrating science, technology, engineering, and mathematics*, Moomaw (2013)

Before we leave this important strategy, let's look at two specific graphic organizers that can help your students work through the process of examining reasoning.

Math Sample: Error Analysis

Name: _____   Date: _____

1. Read the mathematics story problem. Look at the student's work and solution. Identify the error and describe it.
2. Solve the problem correctly. Then share a strategy this student could use to prevent the same error in the future.

Identify error or describe it.

Solve the problem. Steps for correction solution:

Share a strategy. Then, write the strategy that was shared with you.

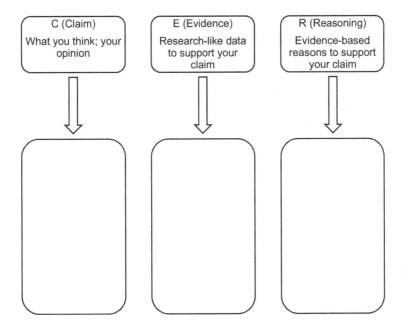

C (Claim) — What you think; your opinion	E (Evidence) — Research-like data to support your claim	R (Reasoning) — Evidence-based reasons to support your claim

Think Like a Mathematician or Scientist

As a part of preparing students for college and careers, it is good practice to teach students how to navigate specialized content. Additionally, thinking mathematically is reflected throughout most national and state standards. Many of us became teachers in our chosen content areas because we enjoyed learning the content, but how well did we truly understand the content? Abbigail remembers the first time her mathematical thinking was challenged. She immediately shut down, but thanks to a persistent teacher who believed she could do it, she became a better mathematics student and a better mathematics teacher. She learned to question her own thinking, reflect and process her thinking like a mathematician.

Why You Should Think Like a Scientist

In the end, the core justification for everything I do in terms of trying to bring science to a broader audience comes back to the idea that science isn't a collection of facts, it's an *approach to the world*. Stripped to its essentials, science is a four-step process: You *look* at something interesting in the world, you *think* about why it might work that way, you *test* your idea with further observations and experiments, and you *tell* everybody what you found.

Source: http://scienceblogs.com/principles/2013/03/20/why-should-you-think-like-a-scientist/

> **How Mathematicians Think**
> ♦ Recognize that all reasoning depends on assumptions.
> ♦ Believe you could be wrong.
> ♦ Value intuition and ideas.
> ♦ Question numbers.
> ♦ Model things.

Source: Josh Bernoff, co-author of *Groundswell* and other books

> **STEM Example**
> **Bracketology and March Madness: Predicting**
> **This Year's Bracket**
> In groups, students will research relevant statistics (including BPI and RPI) for each of the sixty-eight ACC teams in order to fill out a bracket for March Madness games and be ready to defend your bracket choices to the class based on statistics.
> Skills incorporated: discourse, collaboration, research
> Content incorporated: appropriate quantities for descriptive modeling, evaluating data-based reports, decision analysis using probability, probability and statistics

Source: Full lesson plan and additional resources: http://edu.stemjobs.com/wp-content/uploads/2016/02/ STEMJOBS_LessonPlan_Bracketology_DIGITAL.pdf

Thinking from the perspective of a mathematician or a scientist focuses students' attention on the nuances of the content area. For example, if a task asks students to analyze a natural disaster, a mathematician will look at the data chronicling the disaster, while a scientist would consider the environmental impact and implications. To expand the analogy, a social scientist (social studies area) would likely consider the political ramifications. Because math and science are very specialized content areas that require technical and analytical understanding, we need to teach students how to process learning from the perspective of a mathematician or scientist.

Characteristics	
Characteristics of Mathematicians	Characteristics of Scientists
Question everything.	Inquisitive; they ask many questions and formulate a hypothesis.
Write in sentences/use clear communication.	Are avid researchers. We don't know it all.
Consider the converse and the contrapositive.	Make predictions (guess with a purpose).
Think about extreme examples.	Create and carry out an experiment to test a hypothesis and predictions.
Create your own examples.	Make improvements to your experiment.
Where are the assumptions used?	Analyze your data and check your assumptions.
Start with the complicated side.	Make data-based assumptions.
Ask, "what happens if . . .?"	Replicate the experiment for validity.
Communicate.	Share results.

Source: Source for Math Information: www.kevinhouston.net/pdf/10-ways-to-think-like-a-mathematician.pdf

Source: Source for Science Information: Adapted from www.wikihow.com/Think-Like-a-Scientist

Younger students are naturally curious. Their constant questioning means they are on their way to being good mathematicians and scientists. All students have the capacity to think like mathematicians and scientists. The more you expect that type of thinking, the more they will demonstrate it and take these skills with them into upper grades. An abbreviated list of characteristics for your students follows. Use the full list as a teaching tool or instructional support.

Characteristics	
Characteristics of Mathematicians	Characteristics of Scientists
Question everything.	Question everything.
Create own examples.	Are researchers (willing to see what happens).
Thinks of another way to solve a problem.	Shares results with others.

Carol Lloyd also developed a model for guiding mathematical thinking, which also applies to science.

Guiding Thinking	
Guiding Question	Explanation
How do you know what you know?	Students use their text or outside resources to support or justify their thinking, e.g., "I need to know or use my understanding of ____ in order to solve this problem."
What is influencing your thinking?	Students analyze their point of view so they understand that there may be various ways to solves a problem. "To solve this problem, I _____."
So what do you now understand? And so why is this concept or practice important?	"So what" statements should help students do two things: understand the content standard and the learning processes they used. The "so why" statements allows students to make real-life connections.

Source: www.thinkingmaps.com/thinking-like-a-mathematician/

A final source that is beneficial for math teachers is Jo Boelar's work on thinking like a mathematician. Her site contains a wide range of resources, but this page of information is particularly helpful: www.youcubed.org/mathematical-mindset-teaching-resources/.

Conclusion

One facet of rigor is that students demonstrate learning at high levels. When you ask rigorous questions, use inquiry-based instruction and require students to think like mathematicians or scientists, use academic discourse and examine reasoning, you will provide those opportunities for students to move beyond providing basic information to showing their understanding at deep levels.

Points to Ponder

- The most important thing learned . . .
- One strategy I want to implement now . . .
- One strategy I want to save for later . . .
- I'd like to learn more about . . .
- I'd like to share with other teachers . . .

6

Assessment

Assessment is a critical aspect of rigorous math and science classrooms. In this chapter, we'll look at the aspects of effective formative and summative assessments.

Effective Formative Assessment

Formative assessments, which are typically informal, take place throughout the instructional process. They should be administered frequently since they provide an immediate assessment of students' levels of mastery.

Dr. Gregory Firm, a former school superintendent, uses the term "informative assessment" because formative assessments are used to inform the teacher and the student of mastery and progress. He describes six characteristics of effective formative assessment. Although he discusses these characteristics related to math, we find them useful for all subject areas.

Source: www.dreambox.com/blog/what-is-math-formative-assessment

Examples of Rigorous Formative Assessments

Let's look at formative assessments that can be used before, during and after instruction. Then, we'll finish with technology options that can support your efforts.

Before Instruction

Entrance Slips

It is often critical to assess where your students are before even beginning a new lesson or unit. Prior to learning about black holes, you may hand each of your students a sticky note as they come into class that day and ask them to write down what they already know (or what they think they know) about how gravity affects time. Or, in a math classroom, prior to a lesson on pi, you ask them to write down what they already know (or what they think they know) about ratios. Each student brings their sticky note up and places it in the K column of a KWL chart. Then, you can scan and group those notes quickly to discover facts they know and misconceptions they have and gauge what they don't know. This chart can be revisited after the lesson to see what students have learned.

Understanding Goals for Learning

Often, we state the standard, objective or learning goal for students and then move into the lesson. In order to assess student understanding, ask students to reword the standard into a question they should be able to answer at the end of the lesson. Identifying and addressing whether students understand the standard itself will help facilitate understanding during the remainder of the lesson.

Observations

An important formative assessment tool for teachers is the use of observations. Observations can be planned, or they can be spontaneous. In an observation, you simply observe what students are doing and take notes for documentation. You may choose to observe for particular instructional behaviors, or you may simply observe to see what happens from a general standpoint. Checklists, which provide a quick way for you to make notes about your observations, can be simple yes/no tallies, or they can have open-ended entries for teachers to add notes.

Sample Mathematics Checklist

Characteristic	*Notes*
Student demonstrates problem-solving ability.	
Student demonstrates persistence while solving problems.	
Student reflects on his/her thinking.	
Student shows applications of learning to real life.	

Time Management Tip

Definitely use a checklist when observing students. If it helps, use a grid so you can put your criteria on the rows and students' names in the columns. This will save time and focus your observation.

Interviews and Conferences

In interviews and conferences, the teacher meets with students to assess understanding of content, either before a lesson to gauge base knowledge or during a lesson for ongoing assessment. For either of these strategies, the teacher plans a series of questions to ask a student about his or her learning. It's also important to stay flexible and adjust questions during the interview or conference. These are probably used most often in writing situations, but they can be used with any subject area.

Sample Conference Questions

Please tell me a little about your work.

What do you think is going well?

What are you struggling with?

Show me an example.

How do you think you can improve on your own?

How can I help you?

What are your next steps?

Anticipation Guides

Anticipation guides can be used to activate prior knowledge of your students, but they also allow insight into student thinking prior to a new text or topic.

Mathematics Example

Agree/Disagree Before the Lesson	Content	Agree/Disagree After the Lesson
	A *right triangle* can be an *isosceles* triangle.	
	A *right triangle* includes one right angle.	
	A *scalene triangle* is one with no equal sides.	

Math Anticipation Example

You can use this anticipation guide similarly in science. For example, you may be getting ready to introduce a lesson on the life cycle of a frog.

Pre-K Example

Agree/Disagree Before the Lesson	*Content*	*Agree/Disagree After the Lesson*
	Frogs can mate on land or in water.	
	The male frog fertilizes the eggs as they are laid.	
	After a frog's eggs hatch, they are called tadpoles.	

In the pre-k example, students can respond by circling a smile face or frown face to let you know if they agree or disagree with the statement. You can also do it orally by asking students to hold up a card with a smile face or a frown face as you read each statement.

	Content	
	Today the weather is sunny.	
	Today there are puffy clouds in the sky.	
	The temperature in class is cooler than outside.	

During Direct Instruction

Formative assessment must take place throughout the learning process. When teachers continuously and routinely take the temperature of the room, they are gathering invaluable, intangible feedback that immediately informs teaching and keeps the instructional loop alive. Don't underestimate the value of simply listening; circulating throughout the room; questioning; and observing body language, confused facials, nodding of heads or off-task behaviors. These are intuitive indicators of whether your students are understanding your content. However, there are more concrete ways to gather data on the level of understanding your students are obtaining.

Sketch It Out/Describe It

Many students enjoy using pictures to demonstrate their learning. In some cases, they will actually demonstrate learning at a higher level than if they write their answers, and for primary students, it is more appropriate. In Sketch It Out, students draw their responses to a prompt.

Mathematics Example

Given the pattern below, draw the next picture in the pattern.

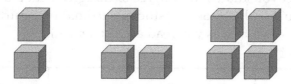

Science Example

Describe in a picture how a plant gets its energy from the sun and turns it into food.

Another option is to provide students with a series of pictures they are required to label and describe. This is particularly helpful when students are in the beginning stages of learning.

What Matters Most

Next, What Matters Most requires students to prioritize information, identifying the most important learning concepts. You can begin by listing information on a chart and having students work together to choose the most important. Over time, they can rank items from most to least important.

I Know . . . I Don't

In I Know . . . I Don't, pairs of students take turns identifying learning concepts they know as well as those they need help with. Note that the students take turns writing what they know or don't know.

I Know . . .	I Don't Know . . .
Partner A writes something he or she knows.	Partner B writes something he or she does not know
Partner A responds to Partner B.	
Switch	
Partner B writes something he or she knows.	Partner A writes something he or she does not know.
Partner B responds to Partner A,	

If neither student knows particular information, they can "ask three before me," meaning they can ask three other students or pairs to help, and then they can ask you if they still need assistance.

Pizza Wheel/Cartwheels

We also like to use a "pizza wheel" to review material that students are assigned to read before class. Rather than simply listing information, using the wheel allows students to visually organize their thinking. Each student writes a fact that he or she learned on one of the pizza slices. Then, working in small groups, students pass their papers to the next group member, who also writes a fact. This continues around the circle until each pizza is full. Students can discuss the material, using the pizza wheels as a prompt.

Pizza Wheel

Student: _____

Topic: _____

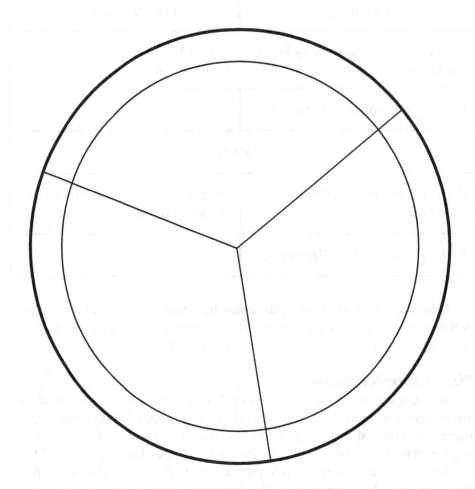

Although you can measure your students' understanding in an oral discussion, asking each student to write his or her response ensures that all students are involved in the lesson and provides an opportunity for every student to respond. The rigor is increased, as each student is required to participate.

One adaptation is Cartwheels, in which each group writes two key points then passes the information to another group who revises, deletes or adds to it. This continues until the information has rotated to all groups.

After Instruction

Exit Slips

Exit slips are an effective way to receive instant feedback on a student's level of mastery.

There are two functions of exit slips, each of which supports different aspects of your instruction.

> ### *Types of Exit Slips*
> ◆ Demonstrate understanding of content
> ◆ Stimulate students' self-awareness
> ◆ Focus on instructional strategies

Demonstrate Understanding of Content

Probably the most common use of exit slips is for students to explain what they learned during the lesson. Although you can simply ask them to write down something they learned, you can also extend that to ask for a higher level of understanding. At the most basic level, simply ask the students, "What are your three take-aways from today's lesson?" It's quite revealing to read what your students actually heard you say that day. You can quickly address misconceptions or reemphasize missed points the next day.

In the example below, students can use a simple thumbs up or thumbs down and drop it in the exit slip box on the way out of the class or at the end of a lesson. The symbols can be placed on a wall or an important space like a bulletin board to help students remember the exit ticket process.

Thumbs Up or Smiley Face	*Thumbs Down or Sad Face*

Stimulate Students' Self-Awareness

In these exit slips, students judge how well they understand the content. For example, you might ask students to rank themselves on a scale of 3 to 1: 3—I can teach this to a partner. 2—I need a little help; if I talk to someone else, I will probably understand this. 1—I'm lost and need help. Ask students, "How would you rate your understanding of what we discussed in class today?" You might place a laminated poster by your door. On the poster, use a picture of a stoplight, mountain or another symbol that is relevant to students. Then, pose the question.

For example, can you identify a triangle among a group of other shapes? Are you able to determine the difference between an acid and a base? Write your name on a sticky note and place it on or near the term or picture that matches your comfort level. If you would like students' responses to be confidential, have them write their choice on a notecard and place it in a box near the door. Younger students may have laminated cards prelabeled with their names, and they can drop it in a designated box.

Sample Responses		
Mountain	*Stoplight*	*Rocket*
Base (Need some help to get started) Climbing the Mountain (I'm making progress) At the Top (I've learned this and am ready to move on to something else) Notice this picture symbolizes that the student will have various moments of success and opportunities to learn.	Red (I'm stuck where I am) Yellow (I need some help before I move on) Green (Ready to move on)	Purple (On the launchpad—ready to learn) Yellow (Firing up the engines—getting started) Green (Everything is fine—I'm where I need to be) Blue (soaring, moving beyond new levels)

Another option is to use *A Bump in the Road*. With a bump in the road, students reflect on their learning and identify two to four points where they hit bumps in the road, or struggles. Then, they partner with another student to see if they can work their way through their struggle.

Focus on Instructional Strategies

When you use an exit slip in this manner, it gives students an opportunity to provide feedback on the effectiveness of specific instructional strategies used to support their learning. This type of exit strategy is best implemented weekly.

> **Sample Prompts for Exit Slips on Instructional Strategies**
> - Did the anchor chart help or hinder your learning during today's lesson? Explain your answer.
> - This week during class, you used an interactive reading guide to help you and your partner process the text. In what ways did this instructional strategy support your learning? In what ways did this instructional strategy hinder your learning?
> - Before we approached the topic for today, we watched a video to provide the background knowledge necessary for understanding the content in our challenging text. To what degree did you find this helpful? How else might we have frontloaded you for the text we read?
> - Today we worked together in small groups to make meaning of the subject matter. How did this facilitate your learning?

No matter what type of exit slip you are using, you'll want to find a way to manage the information. With today's technology, there are many ways to collect exit slip information from your students. With any mobile device, students can access a digital platform and immediately push answers out to the teacher, who then has the ability to display the class's thinking as a whole on the screen or choose a select few to further discuss.

> **Electronic Exit Slips**
> - Google forms
> - Mentimeter
> - Recap
> - Backchannel Chat
> - Plickers
> - Twitter
> - Geddit
> - Poll Everywhere
> - ExitTicket
> - Lino
> - Padlet (will soon require a fee)

Do This . . . Not That

Another way to ask students to demonstrate their understanding of a learning strategy is to use Do This . . . Not That. After learning a new strategy, students complete a two-column chart, explaining what you should do when using the strategy and what you should not do.

	Do This	*Not That*
Mathematics— Justifying a Mathematics Solution	First, state what you did to solve the problem. Second, use mathematical vocabulary to prove why your answer works. Be clear. Third, if necessary, draw a model to show your reasoning.	Give a general answer such as: *"My problem is correct because it looks right."*
Science— Conducting a Science Experiment	Use the inquiry process. Document everything you observe. Record your data and put it in a safe place.	Use your opinion to justify a scientific claim such as: *"I know that dropping ice in boiling water will drop the water temperature and cause the boiling to stop because I saw it happen."*

Utilize Technology Resources

In today's technology-rich society, it's important to incorporate tech-based resources into our formative assessment.

Blogging

Blogging is a unique way to capture student thinking that allows them to process what they learned in a trendy manner. The blog is only used for classroom instructional purposes, but they can invite others to access it. As the teacher, you have full access to the blog as well. You may consider one blog assignment as suggested problem-solving strategies related to different areas of math, whereas another blog entry might require students to contemplate what might have happened if the landing on the moon had failed. While this formative assessment tool may take longer for the teacher to evaluate, it provides an authentic snapshot of what each student is thinking in a modality that fascinates them. You may also allow students to create a vlog, or a video blog.

Screencasting

It's also important to assess what is happening with students' use of technology during instruction. Screencasting allows students to record what happens on a particular device screen and add narration to the recording to make a video file. They can take simple screenshots or collect more extensive information. This process allows you to see and hear their learning process, which gives you a deeper understanding of what is happening.

Video and Audio

Another option is to ask students to use either audio or video to record their thinking. Rather than simply seeing the final answer from a student, you are able to understand where they may have made a mistake, which allows you to help them learn at a higher level.

Other Tools

There are many other tools that allow you to incorporate formative assessment in your classroom. Let's look at a sampling.

Formative Assessment Tools	
Online Platform	*Functions*
Padlet	Acts as digital KWL that can be used to gather student feedback
Socrative	Develop quizzes and exit tickets, use before or after instruction, organizes data for teacher analysis
Backchannelchat.com	Pause during a lesson or reading of a text and ask everyone to comment/respond to a question or prompt.
Nearpod.com	Push content out to student devices, one screen at a time, and allow them to interact digitally through multiple choice, open-ended response, annotating text online, drawing on a blank canvas, explore a virtual 3D image, etc; provides a way for teachers to facilitate a lesson and get immediate real-time feedback as to what your students are thinking

Formative Assessment Tools	
Online Platform	Functions
EdPuzzle	Use any video from a myriad of online sources and insert pause points where students must gather thoughts, answer a question, make a prediction, etc. before they can continue the video; customize a student-directed video lesson and gather feedback via student responses in real time
Explaineverything. com	Watch your students' thinking via this interactive whiteboard that asks students to explain their thinking through a problem or through a prompt; focus on quality over quantity
Flipgrid	Use any IOS device to create a video response to a question or prompt; allows you to see what students know via explanation
Kahoot	Use gaming to review! Game based but allows teachers to create content and disaggregate data
Go Formative	Upload documents, create your own questions, embed videos or pictures, receive immediate data on student performance

Rigorous Summative Assessments

Summative assessments are typically used at the end of a chapter, unit or topical study to assess students' overall understanding. They also form the basis for grades, particularly those used to compute a final grade for the report card. Although they can be used for diagnostic information, they differ from formative assessments in that their focus is different.

Matching Questions

Matching tests are a quick, easy way to assess a wide range of student knowledge. However, it is difficult to assess at a higher level of rigor, as most matching tests measure basic recall questions. Depending on the items, students can guess rather than truly demonstrate understanding.

What are the best strategies for developing quality matching tests? First, make sure there is one best option for each item you list. Ensure that students can see why the items match so there is clear evidence students understand the link. Also, provide more examples than matching items. For example, if you have a list of vocabulary terms and then definitions, add one or two extra definitions to increase the rigor.

Sometimes you need to ask less rigorous questions, but if you use an expanded matching format, in which you create three columns that must be matched, it allows you to increase the rigor. It provides a better opportunity to measure what students know. In this case, you'll also want to provide more choices than items, which requires students to narrow down the answer.

Math Headings for Three-Column Matching Test		
Geometry		
Shape	Name	Description (ex: four sides, all right angles)

Science Headings for Three-Column Matching Test		
Forces and Interactions or Forces and Motion		
Type of interaction example: magnetic	**Example of interaction** Two magnets being attracted to each other	**Example of cause and effect relationship** The way the magnets touch affect their attraction, opposite poles attract

With primary students, you can have them match by drawing lines from a word to its matching picture, and then they can illustrate their own example. See the following example. The chart is only used to illustrate the idea, but you can use it if you have early readers.

Counting Numbers 1. Match the numbers in column A with the correct picture in Column B. 2. In Column C, write a math sentence where the result is the numbers in column A.		
Column A	**Column B**	**Column C**
3 8 5		

True-False Tests

True-false tests are an excellent way for students to determine the accuracy of a statement, agree with opinions and define terms. As with matching items, they are graded quickly and easily, and students can answer a wide range of questions in a short amount of time. However, once again, questions are typically low-level recall questions, and you may not be sure students understand the question or if they are simply guessing. To combat this and to increase the rigor, require students to rewrite any false choices as true statements, which does require them to demonstrate a true understanding of the content. Keep in mind that your questions should also be at a rigorous level rather than requiring rote memorization of knowledge.

Science: Movement of the Moon True-False Test
The moon is important because it affects gravitational pull on Earth. The moon's movement is also affected by the Earth, which causes the different phases of the moon. The phases of the moon are different depending on the time of day, and the phases are what control the tide.

(Note that these statements are false.)

Source: Adapted from: www.quora.com/Why-is-static-friction-directly-proportional-to-the-reaction-force

---

Math True-False Test
2 feet = 1 meter

The student would need to use text to explain that 3 feet = 1 meter.

For primary students, simply ask them to tell you what would make the statement true. The moon is only out during the day. If they understand the lesson at a deeper level, they will know that the moon is always out; we just don't see it. If you happen to see it during the day, use this as a teachable moment and take your children outside to observe.

Multiple-Choice Tests

Multiple-choice tests are probably the most commonly used tests in classrooms across the nation, and they have several benefits. Although due in part to preparation for standardized tests, they are also easy to score. They also apply to a wide range of cognitive skills, including higher-order-thinking ones. Finally, incorrect answers, if written and explained correctly, can help you diagnose a student's problem areas. Disadvantages include that the questions can't measure a student's ability to create or synthesize information and that students can guess an answer.

There are three ways to write multiple-choice questions that allow you to increase the rigor. First, choose a question that moves beyond basic recall. Next, create choices for the stem that are clearly correct or incorrect without making them too easy. In other words, if we provide examples that are clearly off topic, it makes it easier for students to guess. Finally, although some teachers do not like to use "all of the above," "none of the above," "a and d" options, or "mark all of the above," we do find they require students to think at a higher level than basic recall. Remember, you know your students; adapt our suggestions so they match your students' needs.

Mathematics Sample: Middle and Upper Elementary

For your playdate on Saturday at your house, you requested a large pizza, which consisted of 12 slices of pizza. You and your 3 friends ate pizza, but you also had ice cream; there are still 4 slices of pizza left. What fraction of pizza did you and your friends eat?

a. 2/3
b. 3/4
c. 8/12
d. 5/8
e. Both B and C
f. None of the above statements are accurate.

Science Example: Upper Elementary

Which of the following could happen if the moon were destroyed?

a. Eclipses would no longer exist.
b. Earth would experience only one season, summer.
c. The tide would be same all of the time.
d. a and b would happen.
e. a and c would happen.
g. All of the above would happen.
h. None of the above would happen.

Short-Answer Questions

Short-answer questions are an expanded form of fill-in-the-blank questions. Responses are not as long as essays, but they usually include more than one sentence. Because students are required to create a response, they are more rigorous than the types of items we've already discussed. You'll need to build rigor into the context of your questions. Although more challenging to grade than matching, true-false, fill-in-the-blank and multiple-choice questions, they are simpler than assessing essay questions.

Mathematics Example

Based on the three groups of numbers, which **best** represents factors of 42? Why?

a. 1, 2, 3, 14, 42

b. 1, 2, 3, 14, 6, 7

c. 1, 42

Science Example

Based on the three examples, which best represents a device to maximize thermal energy? Why?

Insulated coffee cup   drinking glass   slow cooker

Essay Questions

Essay questions are one of the most common assessments used in today's classrooms. Essay questions are extremely effective for measuring complex learning. Opportunities for guessing are removed, so you can truly measure what students understand. There are several disadvantages, including the amount of time to grade them, the subjective nature of grading and the dependency of the answer on the student's writing ability.

When you are writing essay questions, crafting the question is particularly important. You want to be sure the complexity of the learning outcome is reflected in a clear, focused manner. It's also important to provide explicit instructions as to your expectations.

As with any questions, you can write items at a lower or higher level. In our case, we want to strive for rigorous questions as much as possible.

> ### *Math Example*
> Write a rule for what happens when you multiply a 1-digit number by 10. Explain why your rule will always work.

> ### *Science Example*
> Animals and other organisms inherit traits from their parents. If a scientist were to create a new flower by breeding a red rose with a sunflower, what traits do you think that flower will have? Justify your answer with what you have learned about genetics and heredity.

Performance-Based Assessments

Performance-based assessments are a type of summative assessment, but they differ from traditional testing. They are focused on students performing in some manner to demonstrate their understanding. Typically, performance-based assessments are more rigorous because students must go in depth to complete the performance, project or portfolio. We have discussed projects and project-based and problem-based learning in Chapter 3. Those provide some exemplars of performance-based assessments.

> ### *Sample Performance-Based Assessments*
> - Debates
> - Simulations
> - Video productions
> - Portfolios

Grading

Grading is one of the most challenging parts of a rigorous classroom. Many of the aspects of grading, such as whether to grade homework, are individual choices for a teacher. No matter your decision, help your parents understand grading. Grading has likely changed since they were in school. As Abbigail explains, on her son's report card, she thought NE meant does not meet expectations; after talking with the teacher, she discovered it means not assessed during this cycle or grading period. She was confused because she was unfamiliar with the terminology and NE was not on the grading key. In addition to sharing information with parents, there are other indicators of effective grading.

Grade According to a Policy

In a rigorous classroom, teachers provide a clear grading policy so that students and parents know what to expect. Ideally, you would work together with teachers at your grade level, in your team or in your department so there is consistency. However, that may not be possible. Grading policies should be communicated early in the school year, ideally in writing. They are also important for all grade levels. Remember to match the language and format of the policy to the level of your students. In many cases, your district or school will have standard policies.

Sample Categories for Grading Policy

- Purpose of grading
- How grades, progress and challenges will be communicated
- How grades are determined (tests, projects, homework, etc.)
- Percentage of overall grade for each item/category (project is 30% of grade)
- Homework (how often you assign it, how it counts, penalties for late work, possibility of redoing assignments)
- Late penalties
- Redo policy
- Items that are not assessed regularly but at particular times
- Ways to communicate with the teacher

Rubrics Are Helpful

Rubrics are written descriptions of the criteria used to grade an assignment. They show students what they are expected to do. We've adapted Todd Stanley's steps to creating rubrics from his book *Performance-Based Assessment for 21st-Century Skills*.

Steps to Creating a Rubric

1. Decide the range of performance.
2. Create categories.
3. Provide descriptors in each category.
4. Have a tiered system of descriptors.
5. Make sure the descriptors are specific and include an emphasis on quality in addition to or instead of quantity.

We have provided a sample rubric for upper elementary students. For primary students, you can use alternative headings such as Not Met, Progressing and Mastered. Keep in mind that rubrics may be distributed to students, or it may simply be a chart for information.

Math Rubric for Homework or Individual Practice Problems		
No Credit (Do Over) *0 Points* **Or Not Met for PreK-2**	*Partial Credit* *2 Points* **Or Progressing for PreK-2**	*Full Credit* *3 Points* **Or Met or Mastered for PreK-2**
Response is missing or incorrect. Work is not shown or misses key steps. Students clearly do not understand the problem.	Response is correct, but work shown may be incomplete. Conversely, work shown may be complete but leads to an incorrect answer. It is likely that the student generally understands the problem.	Response and work shown is thorough and correct. Student demonstrates a full understanding of the problem with no mistakes when solving the problem.

Science Rubric			
	Needs Help	*Progressing*	*Mastery*
Use of Scientific Tools	Has trouble choosing the correct tools and using them to gather and analyze data.	Usually chooses the correct tools and uses them to gather and analyze data.	Consistently chooses the correct tools and uses them proficiently to gather and analyze data.
Scientific Process	Completes teacher driven investigation, shows some scientific reasoning but mostly opinion-based, appropriate representations and notations are not used, results are communicated with some assistance	Conducts investigation with little assistance from teacher, demonstrates mostly scientific reasoning by supporting claims, representations and notations are included and are communicated clearly	Plans and conducts own investigation, demonstrates scientific reasoning by supporting claims, representations and notations are detailed, results are communicated accurately and clearly
Scientific Content	Partial or no evidence of an understanding of science concepts, principles, theories and connections.	Demonstrates understanding of science concepts, principles, theories and connections that allows student to apply the learning.	Demonstrates a complex understanding of science concepts, principles, theories and connections that allows student to extend the learning.

Align Grading to Standards

It's important to align your grading to your standards, goals and objectives. That may sound basic, but I've often seen an assignment that called for certain outcomes based on the standards, but the grade was based on other criteria. How frustrating for a student. For example, I spoke with one teacher who assigned her students a written extended response to a question. When she graded it, however, the items that were allocated the most points were neatness and spelling. Whether the student actually answered the question and provided evidence for the response were small portions of the grade. This isn't fair to students. You can count those items, but the main focus of your grade should be whether it meets the standards, goals and objectives.

Example	
Standard: (insert your own)	
Do This . . .	*Not This . . .*
1. Thoroughly read and understand the purpose of the standard. 2. The verb is important but pay close attention to what comes after the verb; that is usually the true depth of the question or standard. 3. Design an assessment that accurately measures the standard. This includes determining the format of the assessment.	1. Skim the standard to understand the main point. 2. Pay attention only to the verb as if nothing else matters. 3. Wait to create your assessment until the end of the unit. Once you have finished teaching, you'll have a better idea of what you want to do.

Don't Count Effort, Behavior or Attendance

One of the mistakes we made as teachers was grading on things that didn't involve the actual work. For example, if a student "tried hard," we gave him or her credit for effort. So as long as he or she attempted to do the work, the student received partial credit, whether or not any of it was correct. This is particularly challenging when we want to encourage feelings of success with younger students, but it's unfair to grade on something other than mastery. What you may choose to do is provide two grades: one for content and one for effort. We've also learned to give students multiple opportunities to complete the work correctly, along with coaching the student, but effort alone does not qualify for a high grade.

Next, we unconsciously graded based on behavior. It wasn't that blatant, of course, but if I had a student who was well behaved and there was a questionable call on the grade, I gave the student the benefit of the doubt. We should have graded equally, no matter what a student's behavior was. But we were inexperienced and didn't realize what we were doing.

Finally, it's easy to incorporate attendance into grading. If a student was absent, we might take points off for each day he or she was late with the assignment. It didn't matter why he or she was absent; our policies demanded points taken off for late work. In effect, we penalized students because they weren't at school. Some had good reasons for missing, some less so. But the bottom line was that we were choosing to grade not on their work but on their presence.

Now we would remove these three factors from grading. A grade should reflect the quality of work, not anything else. However, as we mentioned earlier, you might use a dual grading system to account for factors other than mastery.

Involve Students in Grading

Students feel more ownership when they are involved in the grading process, so involve them in the grading process. Be sure they understand what the grade represents, have them look at samples and grade the items themselves, ask them to self-assess their work and let them create rubrics. In one classroom, the students determined the levels for rubrics.

> ### *Student-Created Categories*
> 4 ... I'm a superhero.
> 3 ... I know what I'm doing.
> 2 ... I'm still working on it.
> 1 ... I need help.

After students create the levels, guide them through the process of what would be an "A" or "B," etc. Student ownership doesn't mean you aren't involved; it simply means you guide the process rather than doing it all yourself. After the rubric is finished, ask students to assess a sample paper so they see how the rubric applies to actual work. Then, revise it together, and you can move forward with its use. It's an excellent way for students to be invested in grading.

Never Give Zeroes

Too often, students don't complete work that requires a demonstration of learning. Typically, this results in a low grade. We often think this means students learn the importance of responsibility, but more often they learn that if they are willing to "take a lower grade or a zero," then they do not actually have to complete their work. For some, that is a preferable alternative to doing work. Perhaps they don't fully understand the assignment, or they may not want to complete it. However, if we truly have high expectations for students, we don't let them off the hook for learning. It's preferable to allow students multiple opportunities to show they understand the learning concepts.

Grade for Quality Not Completion

Be sure that your grade reflects the quality of the work, not just completion or the quantity of included items.

Quality Indicators	Completion Indicators
Depth of understanding Detailed explanation Choice of best or most effective strategy to solve a problem or answer a research question	Completed assignment Included explanation A strategy is used to solve a problem or answer a research question

Conclusion

Assessments are a crucial part of a rigorous classroom. In addition to incorporating regular formative assessment throughout your lessons, you'll want to revise or write summative assessments that move beyond basic questions that allow students to simply guess an answer rather than demonstrating understanding.

- The most important thing learned . . .
- One strategy I want to implement now . . .
- One strategy I want to save for later . . .
- I'd like to learn more about . . .
- I'd like to share with other teachers . . .

7

Collaborating to Improve Rigor

An important part of raising the level of rigor in your classroom and school is collaborating with other teachers. There are various options and purposes for working together. Many teachers are members of professional learning communities (PLCs). The term has become so commonplace that it can mean any type of collaboration. The original meaning of a professional community of learners reflected the commitment of teachers and leaders who continuously seek to grow professionally and act upon their new learning.

Characteristics of PLCs

There are three defining characteristics of PLCs. First, professional learning communities are focused on student learning. As DuFour, DuFour, Eaker, and Many (2006) promote, the goal is to improve student learning by improving what you do in the classroom. Next, there is a culture of collaboration among the participants. You've probably worked in or seen a team of teachers who were assigned to a task, each performed his or her part of the task, and then they walked away. That's not a true PLC. In a PLC, teachers collaborate to move beyond tasks and learn together. Finally, professional learning communities focus on results, no matter what it takes. Although there may be a discussion of challenges, they are not used as excuses.

Benefits of Professional Learning Communities

There are many ways professional learning communities provide advantages for teachers. Opportunities for collaborative inquiry and the learning related to it allow teachers to develop and share their learning. The ultimate benefit of a professional learning community is a positive impact on learning for everyone—including students.

Benefits for Teachers

- Reduced isolation
- Increased commitment to mission and goals of the school
- Collective responsibility for students' success
- Likelihood of professional renewal
- Higher satisfaction, higher morale, lower rates of absenteeism
- Commitment to making significant and lasting changes
- Greater likelihood of undertaking systemic change
- Enhanced learning that defines good teaching and classroom practice
- Creation of new knowledge and beliefs about teaching and learners

---

Source: Adapted from Hord and Sommers (2008); DuFour and Marzano (2011).

Types of Professional Learning Communities

There are many different types of collaborative teams. The choices for collaborative teams can be used to determine which option best fits your needs.

Options for Collaborative Teams	
Option	*Description*
Faculty-wide teams	Participation of the entire faculty in teams focused on the same issue
Interdisciplinary teams	Teams across grade or content areas or that share common planning time or the same students
Grade-level teams	Focus on students at a single grade level
Vertical teams	Working together across grade levels
Subject-area teams	Focus within a single content area
Special-topic teams	Teams formed around topics of interest
Between-school teams	Teachers from more than one school work together

Source: Adapted from: *Team to teach: A facilitator's guide to professional learning teams.* National Staff Development Council, 2009

Scheduling Time for Professional Learning Communities

Successful professional learning communities provide time for you and other teachers to work together to meet, talk about rigor in your school and identify strategies for making your classroom more rigorous. Although you may not have control over scheduling in your school, these ideas provide a starting point for a discussion with school and district leadership.

Providing Collaborative Time	
Strategy	*Description*
Common planning	When teachers share a common planning period, they may use some of the time for collaborative work.
Parallel scheduling	Special teachers (PE, music, art, etc.) are scheduled so that grade-level or content-area teachers have common planning.
Shared classes	Teachers in more than one grade or team combine their students into a single large class for specific instruction, and the other teachers can collaborate.
Faculty meeting	Find other ways to communicate the routine items shared during faculty meetings and reallocate that time to collaborative activities.
Adjust start or end of day	Members of a team, grade or entire school agree to start their workday early or extend their workday one day a week to gain collaborative time.
Late start or early release	Adjust the start or end of the school day for students and use the time for collaborative activity.
Professional development days	Rather than traditional large-group professional development, use the time for teams of teachers to engage in collaborative work.

Are You Ready?

Before we discuss options for PLCs, let's take a moment to self-assess your willingness to participate in a professional learning community. A PLC requires a commitment, and it's important that you participate in the process with a full understanding of what you need to do.

Self-Assess Your Willingness to Participate in a PLC	
Willingness to Participate in a PLC	*Yes/No (Why or Why Not)*
I want to use my knowledge and skills to help other teachers.	
I want other teachers to share their knowledge and skills to help me improve my teaching.	
I am willing to participate in and promote open, honest communication.	
I will participate in a collaboration that is focused on improving student learning, building shared knowledge about best practice and making a difference in terms of results.	
I will honor my commitments to members of my PLC.	
I want to analyze student work at a higher level, set goals based on that data and implement effective teaching practices to meet those goals.	
I am willing to try and adapt new instructional practices, even if they are not successful the first time.	
I will help establish team goals, norms and protocols to ensure collaborative work and participate in adjustments needed to ensure this focus.	

Activities for Professional Learning Communities

Let's turn our attention to the types of activities PLCs can use to impact student learning. We'll look at five options.

Five Types of Activities

1. Learning walks
2. Lesson studies
3. Charette
4. Technology-based options
5. Discussions

Learning Walks

Although we sometimes think that learning walks are for administrators, we are recommending that teachers participate in learning walks. They are not evaluative; rather, they are designed to help teachers learn from each other. Additionally, the goal is to identify areas of instructional strengths as well as possible challenges. You may also want to begin by looking only for positive examples in order to build trust.

A school in Chicago organized "I Spy" days. Teachers dropped in on classrooms for five to ten minutes in order to identify positive examples of instruction. Teachers came back together after school with their "detective notebooks" to share what they had seen. It was an invigorating experience for teachers, who said this was the first time they had had a chance to look at other classrooms. As one teacher explained, "I don't get time to visit other teachers' classes. I learned so much, and I have two new ideas I want to implement tomorrow."

> **Learning Walk Guidelines**
> 1. Work together to identify the purpose of the learning walk.
> 2. Determine the process including length of classroom visits as well as what will occur during the visits. Develop and use a consistent tool for participants to use to record their observations and collect data.
> 3. Inform everyone when the learning walks will occur.
> 4. Conduct a prewalk orientation for those participating.
> 5. Conduct the learning walk and spend no more than five minutes in each classroom. Depending on the lesson, talk with the teacher and students, look at student work and examine the organization of the classroom.
> 6. Immediately after the walk, ask participants to meet and talk about the information they gathered and how to share it with the faculty. They may develop questions that they would ask to learn more about what is occurring.
> 7. Develop a plan for sharing the information and for using it to guide your continued school-improvement work.

Lesson Studies

A more formal option than simply working together to craft a lesson, lesson studies emphasize working in small groups to plan, teach, observe and critique a lesson. It's an excellent reflection of the principles of professional learning communities, as the goal is to systematically examine your teaching in order to become more effective.

In a lesson study, teachers work together to develop a detailed plan for a lesson. One member of the group teaches the lesson to his or her students while other members of the group observe. Next, the group discusses their observations about the lesson and student learning.

Teachers revise the lesson based on their observations, then a second group member teaches the lesson, with other members once again observing. Then, the group meets to discuss the revised lesson. Finally, teachers talk about what the study lesson taught them and how they can apply the learning in their own classroom.

Cycle for Lesson Studies

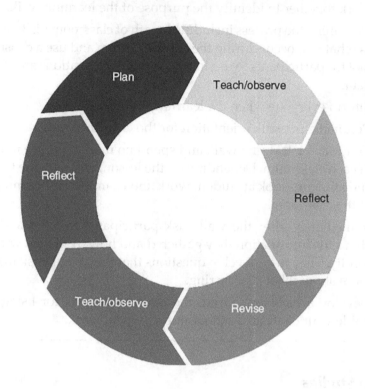

Charrette

A "charrette" is a set of agreed-upon guidelines for talking with colleagues about an issue. The conversation tends to be more trusting and more substantive because everyone knows the guidelines in advance. Charrettes are often used to improve the work while the work is in progress and are not to be used as an evaluative tool. You may be wondering how this differs from a general discussion of an issue. A charrette is typically used when there is a specific issue a teacher needs to address, which at times may have the potential for dissension and therefore needs a more structured approach to the conversation. Additional information about the charrette is available at http://schoolreforminitiative.org/doc/charrette.pdf.

Charrette Protocol

1. A group or an individual from the group requests a charrette when they want others to help them resolve an issue. Often, they are at a "sticking point," and the conversation will help them move forward.

2. Another small group is invited to look at the work, and a facilitator is used to moderate the discussion.

3. The requesting group presents its work and states what is needed or desired from the discussion. The conversation is focused by this presentation.

4. The invited group discusses the issue, and the requesting group listens and takes notes. The emphasis is on improving the work, which now belongs to the entire group. "We're in this together" characterizes the discussion.

5. Once the requesting group gets what it needs, it stops the process, summarizes what was learned, thanks participants and returns to work.

Source: Adapted From: "Charrette Protocol," written by Kathy Juarez and available on the *School Reform Initiative* website (http://schoolreforminitiative.org/doc/charrette.pdf).

Technology-Based Options

There are a variety of ways that teachers are using technology to enhance their PLCs.

Many teachers use Google Docs to share work samples and lesson plans and wikis to share collaborative work. Others use videos to enhance their opportunities to observe and discuss teaching strategies. Sites such as the Teaching Channel provide informational videos but also provide classroom demonstrations. These allow you to watch and critique teaching without visiting an actual classroom.

With the popularity of social media sites, many districts take advantage of that interest. One strategy is to use Twitter chats. Chatham County, in North Carolina, sets a regular time for chats, and they invite experts in the designated focus area to participate. This allows teachers to interact and ask more questions than in the traditional model of training.

Monique Flickinger, director of instructional technology of Poudre Schools in Colorado, shares how her district uses Facebook.

> We created a Facebook account, TeachTechPSD, where we post weekly updates on new technology, pictures of classes using tech and other fun things we are learning about. When teachers come to training with us, we ask them to 'like' us so that, when they check their own accounts, they will quickly see what we are up to.

Discussions

Collaborative discussions are at the heart of a professional learning community. Oftentimes, we think that we can simply "get together and talk." However, we have all participated in group discussions that were derailed by off-topic discussions, meetings that devolved into complaint sessions or times when the discussion was fragmented and the goals of the group were not met.

It Begins With Norms

A crucial part of any effective meeting is having a set of meeting standards or operational norms. This includes basic decisions such as the seating arrangements. If you want an open discussion, try to arrange for participants to face each other, perhaps around a table or in a semicircle rather than in rows. Set firm start and end times and stick to them. This shows that you respect the participants' time. If the meeting is lengthy, plan for a break, but again, set a time and adhere to that. Be sure that any speaker knows his or her allocated time and stays within those parameters.

Ask yourself, "How will we maintain our group memory of discussion and decisions?" Do you want to use charts posted visibly in the room, or will you have someone record notes? In today's age of technology, how can you utilize the equipment you have to support the process? You might even consider recording the meeting. A public recording provides visual clues, develops shared ownership, minimizes repetition, reduces status differences among participants and makes accountability easier.

What are the guidelines for discussion? We often use a "parking lot," which is simply a poster in the room. Participants are given sticky notes, and if there is a question or discussion item that is off the topic, they write it on a note and post it in the parking lot. You can revisit those items at the end of the meeting if there is time, or you can discuss them individually or at another time.

It's also important for everyone to model collaborative discussion. Allowing adequate wait time in response to questions, asking open-ended questions and giving everyone a chance to speak are the foundational elements of a collaborative discussion. Garmston and Wellman (2013) describe seven norms of collaboration that are helpful as you facilitate discussions.

Seven Norms of Collaboration

1. **Pausing:** Pausing before responding or asking a question allows time for thinking and enhances dialogue, discussion and decision making.

2. **Paraphrasing:** Using a paraphrase starter that is comfortable for you, such as "As you are . . ." or "You're thinking . . ." and following the starter with a paraphrase assists members of the group to hear and understand each other as they formulate decisions.

3. **Probing:** Using gentle, open-ended probes or inquiries such as, "Please say more . . ." or "I'm curious about . . ." or "I'd like to hear more about . . ." or "Then, are you saying . . .?" increases the clarity and precision of the group's thinking.

4. **Putting ideas on the table:** Ideas are the heart of a meaningful dialogue. Label the intention of your comments. For example, you might say, "Here is one idea . . ." or "One thought I have is . . ." or "Here is a possible approach . . ."

5. **Paying attention to self and others:** Meaningful dialogue is facilitated when each group member is conscious of self and of others and is aware of not only what he or she is saying but also how it is said and how others are responding. This includes paying attention to learning style when planning for, facilitating and participating in group meetings.

6. **Presuming positive intentions:** Assuming that others' intentions are positive promotes and facilitates meaningful dialogue and eliminates unintentional put-downs. Using positive intentions in your speech is one manifestation of this norm.

7. **Pursuing a balance between advocacy and inquiry:** Pursuing and maintaining a balance between advocating a position and inquiring about one's own and others' positions help the group become a learning organization.

Source: Garmston and Wellman (2013).

Types of Discussions

As we said before, the bulk of time in a professional learning community is spent simply discussing topics and issues. That's why we looked at norms that will help you have effective discussions. Now we'll turn our attention to the types of discussions that typically occur. We've found that most discussions fit in three categories.

Focus on Instruction

First, discussions can focus on instruction. It is important to determine a more focused topic rather than just generally discuss the broad issue of instruction. Within instruction, you may emphasize standards and their relationship to instruction, instructional strategies, relating assessment to instruction or differentiating instruction with the goal of making any needed adjustments that will increase student learning. These areas are not in any particular order; choose the area that meets your needs and that makes the most sense.

Ideas for Discussion	
Focus Area	*Ideas for Discussion*
Standards	Analyze standards to determine exactly what they mean.
	Determine if current instruction addresses standards on a surface level or a deeper level. Determine how standards relate to prior year and upcoming year.
	Determine if particular standards need more or less emphasis.
	Determine any sequence issues. Determine if there are any particular strategies or assessments that would be particularly effective with certain standards.

Ideas for Discussion	
Focus Area	*Ideas for Discussion*
Strategies	Analyze current instruction to determine if it is rigorous and if it leads to student growth (perhaps through a review of lesson plans or learning walks). Assess whether instructional strategies are effective, or if there are other strategies that would be more effective. Research and share any new instructional strategies. Determine whether specific instructional strategies are effective for particular groups of students, such as English learners. Research instructional strategies that are effective for particular groups of students, such as English learners (link to differentiation discussions).
Assessment	Analyze how or if current assessments measure all aspects of instruction, including matching the standard. Determine if there are ways to hone assessments to better match standards or instruction. Research and share any new assessment ideas. Assess the rigor of current assessments. Determine if there are areas of instruction and assessment that either do or do not prepare students for any standardized testing. **For all assessments, consider both formative and summative assessments.
Differentiation	Analyze current instruction and assessment (possibly through lesson plans and written tasks) for differentiation. Determine if there are specific groups of students (such as students with special needs or gifted learners) who need differentiation. Research and share differentiation strategies. Develop differentiation strategies and activities to implement in lessons.

*Source: **Discussions should always lead to appropriate adjustments to impact student learning.*

Focus on Assessment

Next, discussions may also revolve around assessment. Oftentimes, you will combine the discussion to address instruction and assessment, such as in the topics I listed in the previous section. However, there are times you will want to specifically focus on the quality of the assessments themselves. Ideally, you will compare the assessments to an outside benchmark of quality, including the level of rigor.

An effective discussion can surround the concept of measuring the level of rigor of specific tasks, projects, tests and other assessments.

Process One for Assessing Tasks, Projects, Tests and Assessments

1. Review and discuss characteristics of rigorous work during one meeting. You may want to review the samples provided in Chapter 3.

2. Before the next meeting, teachers choose one sample assessment, reflect on the rigor individually and make any desired adjustments.

3. At the second meeting, teachers distribute copies of their sample assessment. Members of the group compare the assignment to the criteria, discuss and come to a consensus as to whether it is rigorous, and suggest any possible changes.

4. Repeat as often as desired.

Another option is to focus on common assessments. In that case, follow the same process, but skip Step 2.

Our preference is to use Webb's Depth of Knowledge as a set of criteria for comparison.

Partial Characteristics of Rigorous Work Based on Webb's Depth of Knowledge	
Math	*Science*
Requires reasoning, planning or use of evidence to solve a problem or algorithm. May involve an activity with more than one possible answer. Requires conjecture or restructuring of problems. Involves drawing conclusions from observations, citing evidence and developing logical arguments for concepts. Uses concepts to solve nonroutine problems.	Requires students to solve problems with more than one possible answer and justify responses. Involves aspects of authentic experimental design processes. Requires drawing conclusions from observations, citing evidence and developing logical arguments for concepts. Involves using concepts to solve nonroutine problems.

Source: Webbalign.org

We've provided you a full sample of all levels of the criteria for each content in Chapter 3. Remember that Levels 3 and 4 are considered rigorous.

Focus on Student Data

When we say "student data," we typically think of test scores. It is certainly important to review students' scores on summative assessments as well as standardized tests. When we do, we can learn about students' strengths and weaknesses, how well they understand content compared to other students and how prepared they are for upcoming lessons. However, we can also learn by looking at work students have completed, whether it is formative or summative work. When you examine and evaluate student work, you can clarify your own standards for work, strengthen common expectations for students or align curriculum across classrooms.

Work Samples to Assess Student Data		
Individual Work Sample	*Group Work Samples*	*Multiple Samples for Different Purposes*
◆ Identify student's strengths ◆ Identify student's weaknesses ◆ Identify growth points ◆ Identify needed steps for improvement ◆ Consider what might have caused this level of work (positive or negative) ◆ Are there any changes needed in the teacher's instruction to support this student?	◆ Focus on patterns ◆ Identify strengths and weaknesses of the majority of students ◆ Identify any areas of growth by the group. ◆ Is any reteaching needed? ◆ Are students ready to move to the next level of learning?	◆ Compare samples from different assessments to look for common patterns ◆ Compare samples from different teachers to determine if a similar level of work occurs in different classes ◆ Compare samples from different teachers to determine if a similar level of work received similar grades ◆ Compare samples from different grade levels to ensure appropriate vertical alignment.

It's important that the discussion is focused on results, not on personalities. At the beginning of the process, agree on a process for the discussion.

Looking at Student Work Protocol

◆ Talk together about the process and how to ensure it is not evaluative.
◆ Identify ways to gather relevant contextual information (e.g., copy of assignment, scoring guide or rubric).
◆ Remove student names and any identifying information.
◆ Select a protocol or guideline for the conversation that promotes discussion and interaction.
◆ Agree on how to select work samples.
◆ Establish a system for providing and receiving feedback that is constructive.

Although there are a variety of guides to use during your discussion, we've provided one for you to consider. Other resources are available at www.lasw.org.

Sample Discussion Guide

- How well do students demonstrate understanding of the standard?
- Is it surface-level understanding or a deeper level?
- Did students complete the work at a satisfactory level? What do we consider satisfactory?
- Are there any particular misconceptions you observe?
- Do students show an understanding of prerequisite knowledge?
- What percentage of students are successful? What do we need to do to help the other students?
- What aspects of the assignment did most students master?
- Which parts did most students not master?
- What does the work of the students tell me about the assignment?
- Is there anything I need to adjust for future assignments?

Assess Your Current Efforts

As we finish our discussion, take time to assess the current status of your professional learning communities. It can be used as a self-assessment or used within your PLC. Once you have completed the assessment, share the results and use them to have a conversation about how to strengthen your work in this area.

Assess Your Professional Learning Community		
Rate your professional learning communities using this scale:		
1—Strongly Disagree 2—Disagree	3—Neutral 4—Agree	5—Strongly Agree

Rating

1. We're organized into collaborative teams to work on curricular and instructional issues.	
2. Collaboration is embedded into our routine practice.	
3. We have agreed-upon indicators or data points that we will use to measure our progress.	
4. We analyze student achievement data to help us establish goals for our work.	
5. We monitor the learning of each student so that we can monitor and adjust our work.	
6. We maintain a "laser light" focus on results.	
7. Each team member is clear about our goals, student expectations and common assessments.	
8. We use the results of our assessments to identify students who need additional time or support and establish processes to ensure that they get the support they need.	
9. We agree to and honor our commitments to members of our collaborative teams.	

10. Our collaboration is focused first on improving student learning.	
11. Our collaboration is also focused on teachers helping others improve.	
12. Our collaborative teams help us build shared knowledge about best practice.	
13. Our teams have established norms and protocols.	
14. Our teams maintain a focus on team goals.	
15. Our collaborative work is monitored and supported.	

Conclusion

If we want to improve our teaching and increase student learning, we will make more progress if we work together. Professional learning communities, when implemented effectively, allow teachers opportunities to participate in activities and discussions focused on improvement.

Points to Ponder

- The most important thing learned . . .
- One strategy I want to implement now . . .
- One strategy I want to save for later . . .
- I'd like to learn more about . . .
- I'd like to share with other teachers . . .

Bibliography

54 Different examples of formative assessment. (n.d.). Retrieved from http://cmrweb.gfps.k12.mt.us/uploads/2/7/3/6/27366965/formative_assessment_ppt.pdf

The Academy of Inquiry Based Learning. (n.d.). Supporting instructors, empowering students, transforming mathematics learning. Retrieved from www.inquirybasedlearning.org

American Museum of Natural History. (n.d.). Curriculum connections: Interactive reading guides. Retrieved from www.amnh.org/explore/curriculum-collections/integrating-literacy-strategies-into-science-instruction/interactive-reading-guides/

Ames, R., & Ames, C. (1990). Motivation and effective teaching. In B. F. Jones and L. Idol (eds.), *Dimensions of thinking and cognitive instruction*. Hillsdale, N. J.: Erlbaum.

Armstrong, A., Ming, K., & Helf, S. (2018). Content area literacy in the mathematics classroom. *The Clearing House: A Journal of Educational Strategies, Issues and Ideas*, 1–11. https://doi.org/10.1080/00098655.2 017.1411131

Atkins, S. L. (2016). *Creating a language rich math class: Strategies and activities for building conceptual understanding*. New York, NY: Routledge.

Barrell, J. (2006). *Problem-based learning: An inquiry approach* (2nd ed.). Thousand Oaks, CA: Corwin Press.

Bender, W. N. (2009). *Differentiating math instruction: Strategies that work for K-8 classrooms*. Thousand Oaks, CA: Corwin Press.

Benjamin, A. (2008). *Formative assessment for English language arts*. New York, NY: Routledge.

Black, P., Harrison, C., Lee, C., Marshall, B., & Wiliam, D. (2004). Working inside the black box: Assessment for learning in the classroom. *Phi Delta Kappan, 86*, 9–21.

Blackburn, B. R. (2008). *Literacy from A to Z: Engaging students in reading, writing, speaking, & listening*. New York, NY: Routledge.

Blackburn, B. R. (2012). *Rigor made easy*. New York, NY: Routledge.

Blackburn, B. R. (2014). *Rigor in your classroom: A toolkit for teachers*. New York, NY: Routledge.

Blackburn, B. R. (2016a). *Classroom instruction from A to Z: How to promote student learning* (2nd ed.). New York, NY: Routledge.

Blackburn, B. R. (2016b). *Motivating struggling learners: Ten strategies for student success.* New York, NY: Routledge.

Blackburn, B. R. (2017). *Rigor and assessment in the classroom.* New York, NY: Routledge.

Blackburn, B. R. (2018). *Rigor is not a four-letter word* (3rd ed.). New York, NY: Routledge.

Blackburn, B. R. (2019). *Rigor and differentiation in the classroom.* New York, NY: Routledge.

Blackburn, B. R., & Armstrong, A. (2019). *Rigor in the 6–12 math and science classroom: A teacher toolkit.* New York, NY: Routledge.

Blackburn, B. R., Armstrong, A., & Miles, M. (2018). Using writing to spark learning in math, science, and social studies. *ASCD Express, 23*(16). Retrieved from www.ascd.org/ascd-express/vol13/1316-blackburn.aspx?utm_source=ascdexpress&utm_medium=email&utm_campaign=Express%2D13%2D16

Blackburn, B. R., & Miles, M. (2019). *Rigor in the 6–12 ELA and social studies classroom: A teacher toolkit.* New York, NY: Routledge.

Blackburn, B. R., & Witzel, B. (2013). *Rigor for students with special needs.* New York, NY: Routledge.

Blackburn, B. R., & Witzel, B. (2018). *Rigor in the RTI/MTSS classroom.* NewYork, NY: Routledge.

Bresser, R., & Fargason, S. (2013). *Becoming scientists: Inquiry-based teaching in diverse classrooms, grades 3–5.* Portland, ME: Stenhouse Publishers.

Buck Institute for Education. (2017). *PBL 101 workbook: The companion to BIE's introductory project based learning workshop.* Novato, CA: Author.

cK-12. (n.d.). Cellular respiration and photosynthesis. Retrieved May 25, 2018, from www.ck12.org/biology/cellular-respiration-and-photosynthesis/lesson/Connecting-Cellular-Respiration-and-Photosynthesis-MS-LS/

Cleary, J. A., Morgan, T. A., & Marzano, R. J. (2018). *Classroom techniques for creating conditions for rigorous instruction.* West Palm Beach, FL: Learning Sciences International.

Cornell Science Inquiry Partnerships. (n.d.). Curriculum for inquiry based resources. Retrieved from http://csip.cornell.edu/Curriculum_Resources/default.html

Diller, D. (2011). *Math work stations: Independent learning you can count on, K-2.* Portland, ME: Stenhouse Publishers.

DuFour, R., DuFour, R., Eaker, R., & Many, T. (2006). *Learning by doing: A handbook for professional learning communities at work.* Bloomington, IN: Solution Tree Press.

DuFour, R., DuFour, R., Eaker, R., & Many, T. (2010). *Learning by doing: A handbook for professional learning communities at work* (2nd ed.). Bloomington, IN: Solution Tree Press.

DuFour, R., DuFour, R., Eaker, R., Many, T. W., & Mattos, M. (2016). *Learning by doing: A handbook for professional learning communities at work* (3rd ed.). Bloomington, IN: Solution Tree Press.

DuFour, R., & Marzano, R. (2011). *Leaders of learning: How district, school, and classroom leaders improve student achievement*. Bloomington, IN: Solution Tree Press.

Dweck, C. (2008). Mindsets and math/science achievement. Prepared for the Carnegie Corporation of New York-Institute for Advanced Study: Commission on Mathematics and Science Education.

Ellis, E. (2004). Makes sense strategies overview. Retrieved June 1, 2018, from www.GraphicOrganizers.com

Ferriter, W. M., & Garry, A. (2010). *Teaching the iGeneration: 5 Easy ways to introduce essential skills with web 2.0 tools*. Bloomington, IN: Solution Tree Press.

Fielding, L., & Roller, C. (1992, May). Making difficult books accessible and easy books acceptable. *The Reading Teacher*, 678–685.

Fisher, D., & Frey, N. (n.d.). Scaffolds for learning: The key to guided instruction. Retrieved June 20, 2017, from www.ascd.org/publications/books/111017/chapters/Scaffolds-for-Learning@-The-Key-to-Guided-Instruction.aspx

Fisher, D., Frey, N., & Lapp, D. (2012). *Text complexity: Raising rigor in reading*. Newark, DE: International Reading Association.

Fleron, J., & Hotchkiss, P. (2014, July). What is inquiry-based learning? Retrieved from www.artofmathematics.org/blogs/jfleron/what-is-inquiry-based-learning

Formative Assessment. (2012). How can I respond to students in ways to improve their learning? A Professional Development Module, Shell Centre, University of Nottingham.

Formative assessment in the mathematics classroom. (n.d.). Retrieved from www.shastacoe.org/uploaded/Dept/ is/County_Curriculum_Leads/2016–17/10–21–16/Formative_ Assessment_in_the_Mathematics_Classroom.pdf

Frey, N. (n.d.). Hands on doesn't mean minds off: Using foldables to promote content learning. San Diego State University. Retrieved from www.boostconference.org/workshop_pdf/Hands%20On%20Doesn%27t%20Mean%20Minds%20Off-Foldables.pdf

Fulwiler, B. R. (2007). *Writing in science: How to scaffold instruction to support learning*. Portsmouth, NH: Heinemann.

Gallagher, J. J., & Aschner, M. J. (1963). A preliminary report: Analysis of classroom interaction. *Merrill-Palmer Quarterly of Behavior and Development, 9,* 183–194.

Garmston, R., & Wellman, B. (2013). *The adaptive school: A sourcebook for developing collaborative groups* (2nd ed.). Norwood, MA: Christopher-Gordon.

Gersten, R., Char, D. J., Jayanthi, M., Baker, S. K., Morphy, P., & Flojo, J. (2009). Mathematics instruction for students with learning disabilities: A meta-analysis of instructional components. *Review of Educational Research, 79,* 1202–1242.

Guido, M. (2017, July). Specific ways to use Webb's Depth of Knowledge in class. Retrieved from www.prodigygame.com/blog/webbs-depth-of-knowledge-dok/

Guskey, T. R., & Bailey, J. M. (2001). *Developing grading and reporting systems for student learning.* Thousand Oaks, CA: Corwin Press.

Hattie, J., & Yates, G. (2008). *Visible learning: A synthesis of over 800 meta-analyses relating to achievement.* New York, NY: Routledge Taylor & Francis Group.

Hattie, J., & Yates, G. (2014). *Visible learning and the science of how we learn.* New York, NY: Routledge Taylor & Francis Group.

Herman, J. (2013). Formative assessment for next generation science standards: A proposed model. *K-12 Center at ETS.* Retrieved May 21, 2018, from www.ets.org/Media/Research/pdf/herman.pdf

Hord, S., & Sommers, W. (2008). *Leading professional learning communities.* Thousand Oaks, CA: Corwin Press.

Hott, B. L., Isbell, L., & Montani, T. O. (2014). *Strategies and interventions to support students with mathematics disabilities.* Overland Park, KS: Council for Learning Disabilities.

Iksan, Z. H., & Daniel, E. (2016). Types of wait time during verbal questioning in the science classroom. *International Research in Higher Education, 1*(1), 72–80.

Inquiry Maths. (n.d.). Inquiry maths. Retrieved from www.inquirymaths.com

Jolly, A. (2017). *STEM by design: Strategies and activities for grades 4–8.* New York, NY: Routledge.

Juliani, A. J. (2015). *Inquiry and innovation in the classroom: Using 20% time, genius hour, and PBL to drive student success.* New York, NY: Routledge.

Lapp, D. (2016). *Turning the page on complex texts: Differentiated scaffolds for close reading instruction.* Bloomington, IN: Solution Tree Press.

Llewellyn, D. (2013). *Teaching high school science through inquiry and argumentation.* Thousand Oaks, CA: Corwin.

Maiers, A., & Sandvold, A. (2011). *The passion-driven classroom: A framework for teaching and learning.* New York, NY: Routledge.

Marshall, J. C. (2013). *Succeeding with inquiry in science and math classrooms*. Alexandria, VA: ASCD.

Marzano, R. J. (2007). *The art of science and teaching: A comprehensive framework for effective instruction*. Alexandria, VA: Association for Supervision and Curriculum Development.

Marzano, R. J. (2010). Giving students meaningful work. *Educational Leadership, 68*(1), 82–84.

Marzano, R. J. (2012). Art and science of teaching: The many uses of exit slips. *Educational Leadership, 70*(2), 80–81.

Marzano, R. J., Pickering, D. J., & Pollock, J. E. (2001). *Classroom instruction that works: Research-based strategies for increasing student achievement*. Alexandria, VA: Association for Supervision and Curriculum Development.

Math Progress Strategies. (n.d.). Graphic organizers. Retrieved from http://teacher.depaul.edu/Documents/Math%20Graphic%20 Organizer%20Guide.pdf

Mathematics Assessment Project. (n.d.). Proving the Pythagorean theorem. Retrieved from http://map.mathshell.org/lessons. php?unit=9325&collection=8

McTighe, J., & Wiggins, G. (2013). *Essential questions: Opening doors to student understanding*. Alexandria, VA: Association for Supervision and Curriculum Development.

Mercer, C. D., Mercer, A. R. & Pullen P. C. (2011). *Teaching students with learning problems* (8th ed.). Upper Saddle River, NJ: Pearson Education.

Michigan Council of Teachers of Mathematics. (n.d.). Rich math tasks. Retrieved from www.mictm.org/index.php/resources/ rich-math-tasks

Moomaw, S. (2013). *Teaching STEM in the early years: Activities for integrating science, technology, engineering, and mathematics*. St. Paul, MN: Redleaf Press.

Moore, C. (2018). *Creating scientists: Teaching and assessing science practice for the NGSS*. New York, NY: Routledge.

Morgan, N., & Saxton, J. (2006). *Asking better questions* (2nd ed.). Ontario, Canada: Pembroke Publishers.

National Association of Colleges and Employers. (2017). Career readiness defined. Retrieved from www.naceweb.org/career-readiness/ competencies/career-readiness-defined/NASA

National Council of Teachers of Mathematics. (2016, July). *High expectations in mathematics Education: A position statement*. Reston, VA: Author.

Neuen, S., & Tebeaux, E. (2018). *Writing science right: Strategies for teaching scientific and technical writing*. New York, NY: Routledge.

Newton, N. (2017). *Math problem solving in action: Getting students to love word problems, grades 3–5*. New York, NY: Routledge.

Newton, N. (2018). *Math workstations in action: Powerful possibilities for engaged learning in grades 3–5*. New York, NY: Routledge.

NGSS. (n.d.). Conceptual shifts in the next generation science standards. Retrieved August 1, 2017, from www.nextgenscience.org/sites/default/files/Appendix%20A%20-%204.11.13%20Conceptual%20Shifts%20in%20the%20Next%20Generation%20Science%20Standards.pdf

O'Conner, K. (2002). *How to grade for learning: Linking grades to standards*. Thousand Oaks, CA: Corwin Press.

Olge, D. (1986). K-W-L: A teaching model that develops active reading of expository text. *Reading Teacher, 39*, 564–571.

Pew Research Center. (2017). U.S. students' academic achievement still lags that of their peers in many other countries. Retrieved from www.pewresearch.org/fact-tank/2017/02/15/u-s-students-internationally-math-science/

Pitler, H., Hubbell, E. R., & Kuhn, M. (2012). *Using technology with classroom instruction that works* (2nd ed.). Alexandria, VA: Association for Supervision and Curriculum Development.

Popham, W. J. (2008). *Transformative assessment*. Alexandria, VA: Association for Supervision and Curriculum Development.

Regier, N. (2012). *Book two: Formative assessment strategies*. Regier Educational Resources. Retrieved May 21, 2018, from www.stma.k12.mn.us/documents/DW/Q_Comp/FormativeAssessStrategies.pdf

Richardson, W. (2010). *Blogs, wikis, podcasts, and other powerful web tools for classrooms* (3rd ed.). Thousand Oaks, CA: Corwin Press.

Sammons, L. (2018). *Teaching students to communicate mathematically*. Alexandria, VA: ASCD.

Sample exit tickets. (n.d.). Retrieved from http://science-class.net/Assessment/Exittickets/exit_tickets.htm

Santa, C., Havens, L., & Macumber, E. (1996). *Creating independence through student-owned strategies*. Dubuque, IA: Kendall/Hunt.

Schlechty, P. (2011). *Engaging students: The next level of working on the work*. San Francisco, CA: Jossey-Bass.

Senn, D., & Marzano, R. (2015). *Engaging in cognitively complex tasks*. West Palm Beach, FL: Learning Sciences International.

Small, M. (2010). *Good questions: Great ways to differentiate mathematics instruction*. New York, NY: Teachers College Press.

Smith, G. E., & Throne, S. (2010). *Differentiating instruction with technology in K-5 classrooms*. Eugene, OR: International Society for Technology Integration.

Solar System Exploration. (n.d.). Retrieved from https://solarsystem.nasa.gov/planets/neptune/overview/

Sparks, S. (2018, March). For teenagers, praising 'effort' may not promote a growth mindset. *Education Week*. Retrieved May 6, 2018, from

http://blogs.edweek.org/edweek/inside-school-research/2018/
03/praising_effort_teenagers_growth_mindset.html#comments

Stanford University. (n.d.). Understanding language. Retrieved from
http://ell.stanford.edu/teaching_resources/math

Swan, M. (2005). Improving learning in mathematics, challenges and
strategies. Department for Education and Skills Standards Unit.
Retrieved from http://tlp.excellencegateway.org.uk/pdf/
Improving_ learning_in_maths.pdf

Swan, M., & Pead, D. (2008). Professional development resources.
Bowland Maths Key Stage 3, Bowland Trust/ Department for
Children, Schools and Families. Retrieved from www.bowland
maths.org.uk

Tate, M. L., & Phillips, W. G. (2011). *Science worksheets don't grow dendrites:
20 Instructional strategies that engage the brain*. Thousand Oaks, CA:
Corwin Press.

Tovani, C. (2011). *So what do they really know? Assessment that informs
teaching and learning*. Portland, ME: Stenhouse Publishers.

University of Pittsburgh. (2013). Supporting rigorous mathematics
teaching and learning: Identifying strategies for modifying tasks
to increase the cognitive demand. Institute for Learning, Tennes-
see Department of Education High School Mathematics TNCore.
Retrieved May 1, 2018, from www.nd.gov/dpi/uploads/1382/
IdentifyingStrategiesModifyingTasksHS.pdf

University of Texas Arlington. (2017, September). How inquiry based
learning can work in a math classroom. Retrieved from https://
aca-demicpartnerships.uta.edu/articles/education/inquiry-based-
learning-math-classroom.aspx

Wiggins, G., & McTighe, J. (2005). *Understanding by design* (Expanded,
2nd ed.). Alexandria, VA: Association for Supervision and Curriculum Development.

Williamson, R. (2012). Research into practice: Importance of high expectations. *Oregon Gear Up*. Retrieved July 12, 2018, from https://
oregongearup.org/sites/oregongearup.org/files/research-briefs/
highexpectations.pdf

Williamson, R., & Blackburn, B. R. (2010). *Rigorous schools and classrooms:
Leading the way*. New York, NY: Routledge.

Williamson, R., & Blackburn, B. R. (2017). *Rigor in your school: A toolkit for
leaders* (2nd ed.). New York, NY: Routledge.

Wyatt, J., Wiley, A., Camara, W., & Proestler, N. (2011). *The development of
an index of academic rigor for college readiness*. Washington, DC: The
College Board.

Zemmelman, S., & Daniels, H. (1988). *A community of writers*. Portsmouth,
NH: Heinemann.

Zikes, D. (n.d.). Foldable and notebook resources. Retrieved from www.dinah.com/

Zikes, D. (n.d.). *Foldables by Dinah Zikes*. New York, NY: Macmillan/Glencoe McGraw-Hill. Retrieved from www.boostconference.org/workshop_pdf/Hands%20On%20Doesn%27t%20Mean%20Minds%20Off-Foldables.pdf

Zikes, D. (n.d.). *Teaching mathematics with foldables*. New York, NY: Glencoe McGraw-Hill. Retrieved from https://blogs.edutech.nodak.edu/badlandsreadingcouncil/files/2012/03/math-foldables.pdf